History of Louis XIV

Makers of History

History of Louis XIV

Makers of History

JOHN S.C. ABBOTT

COSIMOCLASSICS

NEW YORK

The king exerted all his powers of persuasion to induce Madame de Maintenon to enter into the same relations with him which Madame de Montespan had occupied. At last she declared, in reply to some passionate reproaches on his part, that she should be under the necessity of withdrawing from the court and retiring to the cloister, rather than continue to expose herself to a temptation which was destroying her peace of mind and undermining her health. Under these circumstances the king had been led to think of a private marriage. At first his pride revolted from the thought. But in no other way could he secure Madame de Maintenon.

—from "The Secret Marriage"

LOUIS XIV.

PREFACE.

WE all live a double life: the external life which the world sees, and the internal life of hopes and fears, joys and griefs, temptations and sins, which the world sees not, and of which it knows but little. None lead this double life more emphatically than those who are seated upon thrones.

Though this historic sketch contains allusions to all the most important events in the reign of Louis XIV., it has been the main object of the writer to develop the inner life of the palace; to lead the reader into the interior of the Louvre, the Tuileries, Versailles, and Marly, and to exhibit the monarch as a man, in the details of domestic privacy.

This can more easily be done in reference to Louis XIV. than any other king. Very many of the prominent members of his household left their autobiographies, filled with the minutest incidents of every-day life.

It is impossible to give any correct idea of the life of this proud monarch without allusion

PREFACE.

to the corruption in the midst of which he
spent his days. Still, the writer, while faithful
to fact, has endeavored so to describe these
scenes that any father can safely read the nar
rative aloud to his family.

There are few chapters in history more re-
plete with horrors than that which records the
" Revocation of the Edict of Nantes." The
facts given are beyond all possibility of con-
tradiction. In the contemplation of these
scenes the mind pauses, bewildered by the reflection forced upon it, that many of the actors
in these fiend-like outrages were inspired by
motives akin to sincerity and conscientiousness.

The thoughtful reader will perceive that in
this long and wicked reign Louis XIV. was
sowing the wind from which his descendants
reaped the whirlwind. It was the despotism
of Louis XIV. and of Louis XV. which ushered
in that most sublime of all earthly dramas, the
French Revolution.

JOHN S. C. ABBOTT.

New Haven, Conn., 1870.

CONTENTS.

ENGRAVINGS.

LOUIS XIV.

CHAPTER I.

BIRTH AND CHILDHOOD.

Marriage of Louis XIII.

LOUIS XIII. of France married Anne of Austria on the 25th of November, 1615. The marriage ceremony was performed with great splendor in the Cathedral of Bordeaux. The bride was exceedingly beautiful, tall, and of exquisite proportions. She possessed the whitest and most delicate hand that ever made an imperious gesture. Her eyes were of matchless beauty, easily dilated, and of extraordinary transparency. Her small and ruddy mouth looked like an opening rose-bud. Long and silky hair, of a lovely shade of auburn, gave to the face it surrounded the sparkling complexion of a blonde, and the animation of a brunette.*

The marriage was not a happy one. Louis

* Louis XIV. et son Siècle.

XIII. was not a man of any mental or physical attractions. He was cruel, petulant, and jealous. The king had a younger brother, Gaston, duke of Anjou. He was a young man of joyous spirits, social, frank, a universal favorite. His moody, taciturn brother did not love him. Anne did. She could not but enjoy his society. Wounded by the coldness and neglect of her husband, it is said that she was not unwilling, by rather a free exhibition of the fascinations of her person and her mind, to win the admiration of Gaston. She hoped thus to inspire the king with a more just appreciation of her merits.

Louis XIII., at the time of his marriage, was a mere boy fourteen years of age. His father had died when he was nine years old. He was left under the care of his mother, Mary de Medicis, as regent. Anne of Austria was a maturely developed and precocious child of eleven years when she gave her hand to the boy-king of France. Not much discretion could have been expected of two such children, exposed to the idleness, the splendors, and the corruption of a court.

Anne was vain of her beauty, naturally coquettish, and very romantic in her views of life.

It is said that the queen dowager, wishing to
prevent Anne from gaining much influence
over the mind of the king, did all she could to
lure her into flirtations and gallantries, which
alienated her from her husband. For this
purpose she placed near her person Madame
Chevreuse, an intriguing woman, alike renowned for wit, beauty, and unscrupulousness.

Quite a desperate flirtation arose between
Anne and little Gaston, who was but nine years
of age. Gaston, whom the folly of the times
entitled Duke of Anjou, hated Louis, and delighted to excite his jealousy and anger by his
open and secret manifestation of love for the
beautiful Anne. The king's health failed.
He became increasingly languid, morose, emaciate. Anne, young as she was, was physically
a fully developed woman of voluptuous beauty.
The undisguised alienation which existed be
tween her and the king encouraged other
courtiers of eminent rank to court her smiles.

Cardinal Richelieu, notwithstanding his ecclesiastical vows, became not only the admirer,
but the lover of the queen, addressing her in
the most impassioned words of endearment.
Thus years of intrigue and domestic wretchedness passed away until 1624. The queen had

then been married nine years, and was twenty years of age. She had no children.

The reckless, hot-headed George Villiers, duke of Buckingham, visited the French court to arrange terms of marriage between Henrietta Maria, sister of Louis XIII., and the Prince of Wales, son of James I. of England. He was what is called a splendid man, of noble bearing, and of chivalric devotion to the fair. The duke, boundlessly rich, displayed great magnificence in Paris. He danced with the queen, fascinated her by his openly avowed admiration, and won such smiles in return as to induce the king and Cardinal Richelieu almost to gnash their teeth with rage.

This flirtation, if we may not express it by a more emphatic phrase, created much heart-burning and wretchedness, criminations and recriminations, in the regal palace. In August, 1628, the Duke of Buckingham, then in England, terminated his wretched and guilty life. He fell beneath the dagger of an assassin. Anne, disdaining all dissimulation, wept openly, and, secluding herself from the gayeties of the court, surrendered herself to grief.

A mutual spirit of defiance existed between the king and queen. Both were wretched.

Estrangement of the king and queen.

Such are always the wages of sin. Ten more
joyless years passed away. The rupture between the royal pair was such that they could
scarcely endure each other. Louis himself
was the first to inform the queen of the news
so satisfactory to him, so heart-rending to her,
that a dagger had pierced the heart of Buckingham. After this they met only at unfre-
quent intervals. All confidence and sympathy
were at an end. It was a bitter disappointment
to the queen that she had no children. Upon
the death of the king, who was in very feeble
health, her own position and influence would
depend almost entirely upon her having a son
to whom the crown would descend. Louis resided generally at the Castle of Blois. Anne
held her court at the Louvre.

A married life of twenty-two years had passed away, and still the queen had no child.
Both she and her husband had relinquished all
hope of offspring. On the evening of the 5th
of December, 1637, the king, having made a
visit to the Convent of the Visitation, being
overtaken by a storm, drove to the Louvre instead of Blois. He immediately proceeded to
the apartments of the queen. Anne was astonished, and did not disguise her astonishment

1—2

THE CASTLE OF BLOIS.

at seeing him. He, however, remained until the morrow.

Soon after this, to the inexpressible joy of the queen, it appeared that she was to become a mother. The public announcement of the fact created surprise and joy throughout the nation. The king was equally astonished and delighted. He immediately hastened to the Louvre to offer the queen his congratulations.

The queen repaired to St. Germain-en-Laye, about six miles from Versailles, to await the birth of her child.   Here she occupied, in the royal palace, the gorgeous apartments in which Henry IV. had formerly dwelt.   The king himself also took up his abode in the palace. The excitement was so great that St. Germain was crowded with the nobility, who had flocked to the place in anxious expectancy of the great event.   Others, who could not be accommodated at St. Germain, stationed couriers on the road to obtain the earliest intelligence of the result.

On the 5th of September, 1638, the king was greeted with the joyful tidings of the birth of a son.   A vast crowd had assembled in front of the palace.   The king, in the exuberance of his delight, took the child from the nurse, and, stepping out upon a balcony, exhibited him to the crowd, exclaiming, " A son ! gentlemen, a son !"

The announcement was received with a universal shout of joy.   The happy father then took the babe into an adjoining apartment, where the bishops were assembled to perform the ordinance of baptism.   These dignitaries of the Church had been kneeling around a temporary altar praying for the queen.   The Bishop of Meaux performed the ceremony.   **A**

Gift of the Pope.

Te Deum was then chanted in the chapel of
the castle. Immediately after this, the king
wrote an autograph letter to the corporation
of Paris, announcing the joyful tidings. A
courier was dispatched with the document at
his highest possible speed.

The enthusiasm excited in the capital surpassed any thing which had ever before been
witnessed. The common people, the nobles,
the ecclesiastics, and the foreign embassadors,
vied with each other in their demonstrations
of joy. A few months after, in July, an extraordinary messenger arrived from the pope, to
convey to the august mother and her child the
blessing of the holy father. He also presented the queen, for her babe, swaddling-clothes
which had been blessed by his holiness. These
garments were exceedingly rich with gold and
silver embroidery. They were inclosed in a
couple of chests of red velvet, and elicited the
admiration of the royal pair.

The France of that day was very different
from that magnificent empire which now stands
in intellectual culture, arts, and arms, prominent among the nations of the globe. The
country was split up into hostile factions, over
which haughty nobles ruled. The roads in the

rural districts were almost impassable. Paris
itself was a small and dirty city, with scarcely
any police regulations, and infested with robbers. There were no lamps to light the city
by night. The streets were narrow, ill paved,
and choked with mud and refuse. Immediately after nightfall these dark and crooked
thoroughfares were thronged with robbers and
assassins, whose depredations were of the most
audacious kind.

Socially, morally, and intellectually, France
was at the lowest ebb. The masses of the people were in a degraded condition of squalid
poverty and debasement. Still the king, by
enormous taxation, succeeded in wresting from
his wretched subjects an income to meet the
expenses of his court, amounting to about four
millions of our money. But the outlays were
so enormous that even this income was quite
unavailing, and innumerable measures of ex-
tortion were adopted to meet the deficit.

The king was so much gratified by the birth
of a dauphin that for a time he became quite
reconciled to his beautiful and haughty queen.
Two years after the birth of the dauphin, on
the 21st of September, 1640, Anne gave birth
to a second son, who took the title of Philip,

duke of Anjou. The queen and her two children resided in the beautiful palace of Saint
Germain-en-Laye, where the princes were born.

A company of French Guards, commanded
by Captain Montigni, protected the castle.
Madame de Lausac was the governess of the
two children. The title by which the king's
brother was usually designated was simply
Monsieur. But for these children of the king,
the crown, upon the death of the monarch,
would descend immediately to Monsieur, the
king's brother. The morals of the times were
such that the king was ever apprehensive that
some harm might come to the children through
the intrigues of his brother. Monsieur lived
in Paris. The king left orders with Madame
de Lausac that, should his brother visit the
queen, the officers of the household should immediately surround the dauphin for his protection, and that Monsieur should not be permitted to enter the palace should he be accompanied by more than three persons.

To Montigni, the captain of the guard, the
king gave half of a gold coin, of which he retained the other half. Montigni was commanded to watch over the persons of the princes
with the utmost vigilance. Should he receive

PALACE OF SAINT GERMAIN EN-LAYE.

an order to remove them, or to transfer them
to other hands, he was enjoined not to obey
that order, even should it be in the handwrit-
ing of his majesty himself, unless he at the
same time received the other half of the broken
coin.

The king, as we have mentioned, had been
for some time in feeble health. Early in the
spring of 1643 he became seriously ill. The
symptoms were so alarming as to lead the
king, as well as his friends, to think that death
could not be far distant. There are few men
so hardened as to be able to contemplate without some degree of anxiety death and the final
judgment. The king was alarmed. He be-
took himself to prayer and to the scrupulous
discharge of his religious duties.

In preparation for the great change, he repaired to Saint Germain to invest the queen
with the regency when he should die. His
brother, Monsieur, who had taken the title of
the Duke of Orleans, and all the leading nobles
of the court, were present. The king, pale,
emaciate, and with death staring him in the
face, was bolstered in his bed. Anne of Austria stood weeping by his side. She did not
love her husband—she did love power; but

the scene was so solemn and so affecting as to
force tears into all eyes. The dauphin was
then four and a half years old. He was declared king, with the title of Louis XIV., under the regency of his mother until he should
attain his majority.

The next day, April 21st, the christening of
the dauphin with his new title took place with
great state in the chapel of the palace. After
the celebration of the rite, the dauphin was
carried into the chamber of his dying father,
and seated upon the bed by his side. The
poor king, dying in the prime of life, was oppressed with the profoundest melancholy.
There was nothing in the memory of the past
to give him pleasure; nothing in the future to
inspire him with well-grounded hope. Turning to the little prince, who had just been chris-
tened with the royal title, he inquired,

"What is your name, my child?"

"Louis XIV.," the dauphin promptly replied.

"Not yet," said the king, sadly, shaking his
head; "but pray God that it may soon be so."

A few more days of sickness and suffering
passed away, during which it was almost hour-
ly expected that the king would die. Death
often comes to the palace invested with terrors

unknown in the cottage.   Beneath his sceptre
all gradations and conditions of rank disappear.   The sufferings of the king were such
that he longed for release. .

On the 13th of May, as the shades of evening were gathering around his dying bed, he
anxiously inquired of his physicians if it were
possible that he could live until morning.
They consulted together, and then informed
him that they did not think it possible.

"God be praised!" the king replied.   " I
think it is now time that I should take leave
of all whom I love."

The royal household was immediately assembled around the couch of the dying monarch.   He had sufficient strength to throw his
arms around the neck of the queen, and to press
her tenderly to his heart.   In such an hour
past differences are forgotten.   In low and
broken tones of voice, the king addressed the
queen in a few parting words of endearment.

The dauphin was then placed in his arms.
Silently, but with tearful eyes, he pressed his
thin and parched lips to both cheeks and to the
brow of the child, who was too young to com-
prehend the solemn import of the scene.

His brother, Monsieur, the duke of Orleans,

the king had never loved. In these later years he had regarded him with implacable hostility. But, subdued by the influences of death, he bade that brother an eternal adieu, with even fond caresses. Indeed, he had become so far reconciled to Monsieur that he had appointed him lieutenant general of the kingdom, under the regency of Anne of Austria, during the minority of the dauphin.

Several of the higher ecclesiastics were present, who had assisted in preparing him to die. He affectionately embraced them all, and then requested the Bishop of Meaux to read the service for the dying. While it was being read he sank into a lethargy, and never spoke again. He died in the forty-second year of his age, after a reign of thirty-three years, having ascended the throne when but nine years old.

Immediately after the death of the king, Anne of Austria held a private interview with Monsieur, in which they agreed to co-operate in the maintenance of each other's authority. The Parliament promptly recognized the queen as regent, and the Duke of Orleans as lieutenant general, during the minority of the dauphin.

The Duke de Grammont, one of the highest

nobles of France, and a distinguished member
of the court of Louis XIII., had a son, the
Count de Guiche, a few months older than the
dauphin. This child was educated as the play-
fellow and the companion in study of the
young king. One of the first acts of Anne of
Austria was to assemble the leading bodies of
the realm to take the oath of allegiance to her
son. The little fellow, four and a half years
old, arrayed in imperial robes, was seated upon
the throne. The Count de Guiche, a very se-
date, thoughtful, precocious child, was placed
upon the steps, that his undoubted propriety of
behavior might be a pattern to the infant king.
Both of the children behaved remarkably well.

Soon after this, at the close of the year 1643,
the queen, with her household, who had resided
during the summer in the palace of the Louvre,
took up her residence in what was then called
the Cardinal Palace. This magnificent building, which had been reared at an enormous expense, had been bequeathed by the Cardinal
Richelieu to the young king. But it was suggested that it was not decorous that the king
should inhabit a mansion which bore the name
of the residence of a subject. Therefore the
inscription of *Cardinal Palace* was effaced

from above the doorway, and that of *Palais Royal* placed in its stead. The palace had cost the cardinal a sum nearly equal to a million of dollars. This ungrateful disregard of the memory of the cardinal greatly displeased his surviving friends, and called forth earnest remonstrance. But all expostulations were in vain. From that day to this the renowned mansion has been known only as the "Palais Royal." The opposite engraving shows the palace as left by the cardinal. Since his day the building has been greatly enlarged by extending the wings for shops around the whole inclosure of the garden.

Louis XIV. was at this time five years old. The apartments which had been occupied by Richelieu were assigned to the dauphin. His mother, the queen regent, selected for herself rooms far more spacious and elegant. Though they were furnished and embellished with apparently every appliance of luxury, Anne, fond of power and display, expended enormous sums in adapting them to her taste. The cabinet of the regent, in the gorgeousness of its adornments, was considered the wonder of Paris.

Cardinal Mazarin had also a suite of rooms assigned him in the palace which looked out

THE PALAIS ROYAL.

upon the Rue des bons Enfans. These households were quite distinct, and they were all
surrounded with much of the pageantry of
royalty. The superintendence of the education of the young prince was intrusted to the
cardinal. He had also his governor, his sub-
governor, his preceptor, and his valet de chambre, each of whom must have occupied posts of
honor rather than of responsibility. The Marchioness de Senecey, and other ladies of high
rank, were intrusted with the special care of
the dauphin until he should attain the age of
seven years.

Thus the court of the baby-king was quite
imposing. From his earliest years he was accustomed to the profoundest homage, and was
trained to the most rigid rules of etiquette.
The dauphin early developed a fondness for
military exercises. Very eagerly he shoulder-
ed the musket, brandished the sword, and beat
the drum. The temperament of his brother
Philip, the duke of Anjou, was very different:
he was remarkably gentle, quiet, and affectionate. Gradually the baby-court of the dauphin
was increased by the addition of other lads.
The young king was the central luminary
around whom they all revolved. By them all

1—3

the dauphin was regarded with a certain kind
of awe, as if he were a being of a superior, almost of a celestial race. These lads were
termed "children of honor." They always
addressed the king, and were addressed in return, with the formality of full-grown men.
One day a little fellow named Lomenie delighted the king with a gift. The king was
amusing himself with a cross-bow, which for
the time being happened to be in special favor.
He loaned the bow for a few moments to Lomenie. Soon, however, anxious to regain the
valued plaything, he held out his hand to take
it back. His governess, the Marchioness de
Senecey, said to him, aside,

"Sire, kings give what they lend."

Louis, immediately approaching his companion, said, calmly, "Monsieur de Lomenie, keep
the cross-bow. I wish that it were something
of more importance; but, such as it is, I give
it to you with all my heart."

This was a speech of a boy of five years old
to a companion of the same age. When the
dauphin reached his seventh birthday, a great
change took place in his household. All his
female attendants were withdrawn, and he was
placed exclusively under the charge of men.

It is said that this change was at first the occasion of much grief to him. He had become much attached to many of the ladies, who had devoted themselves to the promotion of his happiness. We are told that he was greatly chagrined to find that none of the gentlemen of his court could tell him any of those beautiful fairy tales with which the ladies had often lulled him to sleep. In conference with the queen upon the subject, it was decided that M. Laporte, his first valet de chambre, should read to him every night a chapter of a very popular history of France. The dauphin soon became greatly interested in the narrative. He declared that he, when he grew up, would be a Charlemagne, a St. Louis, a Francis First, and expressed great abhorrence of the tyrannical and slothful kings.

The pleasure which the little king took in these historical readings daily increased. Cardinal Mazarin accidentally found out what was going on, and was greatly displeased. He was anxious that the intellectual powers of the king should not be developed, for the cardinal desired to grasp the reins of government with his own hands. To do this, it was necessary that the king should be kept ignorant, and should be incited only to enervating indulgence.

Scornfully the cardinal remarked, " I pre-
sume the governor of the king must put on his
shoes and stockings, as I perceive his valet de
chambre is teaching him history."

The young king entertained an instinctive
aversion to the proud cardinal, who assumed
imperial airs, and who was living in splendor
far surpassing that of the regent or of the child
king. Those who surrounded the prince were
equally inimical to the cardinal-minister, who,
in that age of superstition and fanaticism, had
attained such power that the regent herself
stood in awe of him.

Henrietta, queen of England, wife of the unfortunate Charles I., was a daughter of Henry
IV., and sister of Louis XIII. She was consequently aunt to the dauphin. The troubles
in England, which soon led to the beheading
of the king her husband, rendered it necessary
for her to escape to France. Her brother,
Monsieur, duke of Orleans, went to the coast to
receive his unhappy and royal sister. As they
approached Paris, the queen regent and her son
the king rode out to meet them. Henrietta
took a seat in the same carriage with their
majesties, and returned with them to the Louvre. The pallid cheeks and saddened features

of the English queen proclaimed so loudly the
woes with which she was stricken as to exert
universal sympathy.

The young king at seven years of age was
tall, muscular, and excelled in all physical exercises ; but the villainous cardinal had endeavored in every way to dwarf his intellect,
so that his mind remained almost a blank.
Both the young king and his brother at this
early age had acquired a very remarkable degree of courtly grace. A chronicler of the
times, speaking of the bearing of Louis at a
court wedding, says,

" The king, with the gracefulness which
shines in all his actions, took the hand of the
Queen of Poland, and conducted her to the
platform, where his majesty opened the dance,
and was followed by nearly all the princes,
princesses, great nobles, and ladies of the court.
At its termination, the king, with the same
grace and majestic deportment, conducted the
young queen to her place. The king then
danced a second time, and led out the Duke
of Anjou with such skill that every one was
charmed with the polite bearing of these two
young princes."

Early in the year 1646, the king, not yet

quite eight years old, was conducted upon what
was singularly called his first campaign. The
queen and her son repaired to Amiens, where
they sojourned for a short time with the army,
and established a very brilliant court. When
the army left Amiens for Flanders, the regent
and her son returned from their campaign.

The infant court of the monarch was now
established at Paris. The ambitious cardinal
had brought from Italy several little children,
his relatives, the eldest of whom had attained
but her twelfth year. They were immediately
introduced to the court of Louis XIV. The
wealth of the cardinal was such, and his influence so great, that, young as these his nieces
were, they were instantly surrounded by ad-
mirers. The Duke of Orleans, who hated the
cardinal and all that belonged to him, bitterly
remarked,

"There is such a throng about those little
girls that I doubt if their lives are safe, and
if they will not be suffocated."

The boy-king, however, notwithstanding his
dislike for the cardinal, received the little girls
with that gallantry for which throughout life
he was distinguished.

Very early he began to develop quite a pos-

itive character. On one occasion the courtiers
were speaking in his presence of the absolute
power exercised by the sultans of Turkey.
Several very striking examples were given.
The young prince, who had listened attentive-
ly, remarked,

"That is as it should be ; that is really reigning."

"Yes, sire," pertinently replied Marshal d'Es-
trees, "but two or three of those sultans have,
within my memory, been strangled."

The Prince de Condé inquired of Laporte,
the first valet of the king, respecting the character his young majesty was developing. Upon
being told that he was conscientious and intelligent, he replied, "So much the better. There
would be no pleasure in obeying a fool, and
no honor in being commanded by a bad man."

Cardinal Mazarin, the prime minister, who
looked with jealousy upon any development of
superior intelligence in the dauphin, said to
Marshal de Grammont, "Ah! sir, you do not
know his majesty. There is enough stuff in
him to make four kings and an honest man."

There had gradually sprung up a deadly
feud between the court, headed by the tyrannical minister Mazarin on the one side, and by

the Parliament on the other. The populace
of Paris were in sympathy with the Parliament. Many of the prominent nobles, some
even of royal blood, detesting the haughty
prime minister, espoused the Parliamentary
cause. There were riots in Paris. Affairs
looked very threatening. Mazarin was alarmed, and decided to escape from Paris with the
court to the palace of St. Germain. There he
could protect the court with an ample military
force. He thought, also, that he should be able
to cut off the supply of provisions from the
capital, and thus starve the city into subjection.

It was necessary to move with much caution,
as the people were greatly agitated, were filling the streets with surging crowds, and would
certainly prevent the removal of the king
should they suspect the design. The night of
the 5th of January was selected as a time in
which to attempt the escape. The matter was
kept profoundly secret from most of the members of the royal household.

At three o'clock in the morning a carriage
was drawn up in the gate of the royal garden.
The queen regent, who, to avoid suspicion, had
retired to bed at the usual hour, had in the
mean time risen and was prepared for her

flight. The young king and his brother were awoke from their sleep, hurriedly dressed, and conveyed to the carriage in waiting. The queen regent, with several other prominent members of the court, descended the back stairs which led from the queen's apartment and joined the children. Immediately one or two other carriages drove up, and the whole party entered them, and by different routes, through the dark and narrow streets, left the city. It was a short ride of about twelve miles.

Other prominent members of the court, residing in different parts of the city, had been apprised of the movement, so that at five o'clock in the morning twenty carriages, containing one hundred and fifty persons, drove into the court-yard of the palace. One of the ladies who accompanied the expedition, Mademoiselle Montpensier, gives the following graphic description of the scene:

"When we arrived at St. Germain we went straight to the chapel to hear mass. All the rest of the day was spent in questioning those who arrived as to what they were doing in Paris. The drums were beating all over the city, and the citizens had taken up arms. The

Countess de Fiesque sent me a coach, and a
mattress, and a little linen. As I was in so
sorry a condition, I went to seek help at the
Chateau Neuf, where *Monsieur and Madame*
were lodged ; but Madame had not her clothes
any more than myself. Nothing could be
more laughable than this disorder. I lodged
in a large room, well painted and gilded, with
but little fire, which is not agreeable in the
month of January. My mattress was laid
upon the floor, and my sister, who had no bed,
slept with me. Judge if I were agreeably situated for a person who had slept but little the
previous night, with sore throat and violent
cold.

" Fortunately for me, the beds of Monsieur
and Madame arrived. Monsieur had the kind-
ness to give me the room which he vacated.
As I was in the apartment of Monsieur, where
no one knew that I was lodged, I was awoke
by a noise. I drew back my curtain, and was
much astonished to find my chamber quite
filled by men in large buff skin collars, who appeared surprised to see me, and who knew me
as little as I knew them.

" I had no change of linen, and my day che-
mise was washed during the night. I had no

women to arrange my hair and dress me, which is very inconvenient. I ate with Monsieur, who keeps a very bad table. Still I did not lose my gayety, and Monsieur was in admiration at my making no complaint. It is true I am a creature who can make the best of every thing, and am greatly above trifles. I remained in this state ten days, at the end of which time my equipage arrived, and I was very glad to have all my comforts. I then went to lodge in the chateau Vieux, where the queen was residing."*

At a very early hour in the morning the news was circulated through the streets of Paris that the court had fled from the city, taking with it the young king. The excitement was terrible, creating universal shouts and tumults. All who were in any way connected with the court attempted to escape in various disguises to join the royal party. The populace, on the other hand, closed the gates, and barricaded the streets, to prevent their

---

* There were at that time two palaces at St. Germain. The old palace, originally built by Charles V., and in the alteration of which Louis XIV. spent over a million of dollars, still remains. The new palace, constructed by Henry IV. about a quarter of a mile from the other, is now in ruins.

flight. In the midst of this confusion, a letter
was received by the municipal magistrates,
over the signature of the boy-king, stating that
he had been compelled to leave the capital to
prevent the seizure of his person by the Parliament, and urging the magistrates to do all
in their power for the preservation of order
and for the protection of property. The king
also ordered the Parliament immediately to
retire from the city to Montargis.

The Parliament refused to recognize the order, declaring "that it did not emanate from
the monarch himself, but from the evil coun-
selors by whom he was held in captivity."
Upon the reception of this reply, the queen regent, who had surrounded her palace at St.
Germain with a thousand royal troops, acting
under the guidance of Mazarin, issued a decree
forbidding the villages around Paris sending
into the capital either bread, wine, or cattle.
Troops were also stationed to cut off such sup-
plies. This attempt to subdue the people by
the terrors of famine excited intense exasper-
ation. A decree was promptly issued by the
Parliament stating,

"Since Cardinal Mazarin is notoriously the
author of the present troubles, the Parliament

declares him to be the disturber of the public
peace, the enemy of the king and the state,
and orders him to retire from the court in the
course of this day, and in eight days more from
the kingdom. Should he neglect to do this, at
the expiration of the appointed time all the
subjects of the king are called upon to hunt
him down."

At the same time, men-at-arms were levied
in sufficient numbers to escort safely into the
city all those who would bring in provisions.
The Parliament, from the populace of Paris,
could bring sixty thousand bayonets upon any
field of battle. Thus very serious civil war
was inaugurated.

As we have mentioned, many of the nobles,
some of whom were allied to the royal family,
assuming that they were not contending against
their legitimate sovereign, the young king, but
against the detested Mazarin, were in cordial
co-operation with the Parliament. The people
in the rural districts were also in sympathy
with the party in Paris.

The court party was now called " The *Maz-
arins*," and those of the Parliament " The
Fronde." The literal meaning of the word
fronde is sling. It is a boy's plaything, and,

when skillfully used, an important weapon of
war. It was with the sling that David slew
Goliath. During the Middle Ages this was the
usual weapon of the foot soldiers. Mazarin
had contemptuously remarked that the Parliament were like school-boys, *fronding in the
ditches,* and who ran away at the approach of
a policeman. The Parliament accepted the
title, and adopted the *fronde* or *sling* as the
emblem of their party.

There were now two rival courts in France.
The one at St. Germain was in a state of great
destitution. The palace was but partially furnished, and not at all capable of affording
comfortable accommodations for the crowd
which thronged its apartments. Nothing could
be obtained from Paris. Their purses were
empty. The rural population was hostile, and,
while eager to carry their products to Paris,
were unwilling to bring them to St. Germain.
Madame de Motteville states in her memoirs
" that the king, queen, and cardinal were sleeping upon straw, which soon became so scarce
that it could not be obtained for money."

The court of the Fronde was assembled at
the Hotel de Ville in Paris. There all was
splendor, abundance, festive enjoyment. The

high rank of the leaders and the beauty of the
ladies gave éclat to the gathering.

Cardinal Mazarin was not only extortionate,
but miserly. He had accumulated an enormous property. All this was seized and ap-
propriated by the Fronde. Though there were
occasional skirmishes between the forces of the
two factions, neither of them seemed disposed
to plunge into the horrors of civil war.

The king sent a herald, clad in complete armor and accompanied by two trumpeters, to
the Parliament. The Fronde refused to receive the herald, but decided to send a deputation to the king to ascertain what overtures he
was willing to make. After a lengthy conference a not very satisfactory compromise was
agreed upon, and the royal fugitives returned
to Paris. It was the 5th of April, 1650. A
Te Deum was chanted with great pomp at the
cathedral of Notre Dame.

"Thus terminated the first act of the most
singular, bootless, and, we are almost tempted
to add, burlesque war which, in all probability,
Europe ever witnessed. Throughout its whole
duration society appeared to have been smitten
with some moral hallucination. Kings and
cardinals slept on mattresses, princesses and

duchesses on straw.   Market-women embraced
princes, prelates governed armies, court ladies
led the mob, and the mob, in its turn, ruled the
city."*

* Louis XIV. and the Court of France, vol. i., p. 262.

CHAPTER II.

THE BOY-KING.

THE reconciliation between the court and the Fronde was very superficial. The old antagonism soon reappeared, and daily grew more rancorous. To add to the embarrassment of the court, *Monsieur*, the duke of Orleans, became alienated from Mazarin, and seemed inclined to join the Fronde. The most formidable antagonist of the cardinal in the Parliament was M. de Retz. He was coadjutor of the Archbishop of Paris, a man of consummate address and great powers of eloquence.

The struggle between De Retz and Mazarin soon became one of life and death. The coadjutor was at length imboldened to offer a decree in Parliament urging the king to banish from his presence and his councils Cardinal Mazarin. This measure threw the court into consternation. The cardinal was apprehensive of arrest. Some of his friends urged him to retire immediately to a fortress. Oth-

1—4

ers proposed to garrison the Palais Royal and its neighborhood with an efficient guard.

From the saloons of the palace the shouts were heard of the excited populace swarming through the streets. No one could tell to what extremes of violence they might proceed. Warned by these hostile demonstrations, the cardinal decided to escape from Paris. At ten o'clock at night he took leave of the queen regent, hastened to his apartments, exchanged his ecclesiastical costume for a dress in which he was entirely disguised, and on foot threaded the dark streets to escape from the city. Two of his friends accompanied him. At the Richelieu Gate they took horses, which were awaiting them there, and in two hours alighted at the palace of St. Germain.

M. de Retz, through his spies, was immediately informed of the flight of the cardinal. He at once hastened to communicate the intelligence to *Monsieur*. The duke at first could not credit the statement, as he felt assured that Mazarin would not have left without taking the young king with him. Should the cardinal, in his retreat, gain possession of the king, in whose name he would issue all his orders, it would be hardly possible to avoid the

horrors of a desolating civil war. All minds
in Paris, from the highest to the lowest, were
thrown into a state of the most intense excitement.

On the night of the second day after the
cardinal's flight, M. de Retz was awakened by
a messenger, who informed him that the Duke
of Orleans was anxious to see him immediately at the palace of the Luxembourg. The coadjutor rose, hastily dressed, and in great anxiety repaired to the palace. The duke, though
lieutenant general of the kingdom, was a very
timid man, and exceedingly inefficient in action. As they entered the chamber of the
duke, he listlessly said to M. de Retz,

"It is just as you said. The king is about
to leave Paris; what shall we do? I do not
see what can be done to prevent it."

The resolute coadjutor replied, "We must
immediately take possession of the city gates."

But the inert and weak duke brought forward sundry silly excuses. He had not sufficient force of character or moral courage to
commit himself to any decisive course of action. The only measure he could be induced
to adopt was to send a message to the queen
regent, imploring her to reflect upon the con-

sequences which would inevitably result from
the removal of the king from Paris.   In the
mean time, the resolute and fearless coadjutor
sent his emissaries in all directions.   The populace were aroused with the cry that Mazarin
was about to carry off the king.   The gates of

PALACE OF THE LUXEMBOURG.

the city were seized.   Mounted patrols trav-
ersed the streets urging the citizens to arms.
An enormous crowd of excited men and wom-
en rushed toward the Palais Royal.

The carriages were, in fact, at that hour, at
the appointed rendezvous for the midnight
flight of the king and his attendants.   The
young monarch was already in his traveling

dress, just about to descend the stairs of the palace, when the queen was apprised, by the tumult in the streets, that the design was discovered, and that consequently its execution was impracticable.

With the utmost precipitancy, the traveling dress of the king was removed, and he was robed in his night garments, replaced in bed, and urged to feign that he was asleep. Scarcely was this accomplished ere one of the officers of the household entered and announced to the queen that the exasperated mob was threatening the palace, insisting upon seeing the king, that they might satisfy themselves that he had not been carried away. While he was speaking, another messenger entered with the announcement that the mob had already proceeded to violence, and were tearing down the palisades of the palace. While he was yet speaking, a messenger from the Duke of Orleans arrived, imploring the queen regent not to attempt the removal of the king, and assuring her that it was impossible to do so, since the citizens were resolved to prevent it.

The queen, with dignity, listened to all. To the messenger of the Duke of Orleans she haughtily replied,

"Say to the duke that he, instigated by the coadjutor, has caused this tumult, and that he has power to allay it. That nothing can be more unfounded than the idea that there has been any design to remove the king. That both his majesty and his brother, the Duke of Anjou, are asleep in their beds, as I myself had been until the uproar in the streets had caused me to rise." To satisfy the messenger, M. de Souches, she led him into the chamber of the king, and showed him his majesty apparently soundly asleep.

As they were softly retiring from the room, the outcry of the populace filling the court-yard was heard shouting "The king! the king! we must see the king." The queen regent hesitated for a moment, and then, with wonderful presence of mind, and with moral and physical courage rarely equaled, turning to the envoy of *Monsieur*, said,

"Say to the people that the doors of the palace shall be immediately thrown open, and that every one who wishes may enter the chamber of the king. But inform them that his majesty is asleep, and request them to be as quiet as is possible."

M. Souches obeyed. The doors were open

ed. The mob rushed in. Nevertheless, contrary to all expectation, they had no sooner
reached the royal apartment than their leaders,
remembering that their king was sleeping, desired the untimely visitors to proceed in perfect quiet. As the human tide moved onward,
their very breathing was suppressed. They
trod the floor with softest footsteps. The
same tumultuous multitude that had howled,
and yelled, and threatened outside the gates,
now, in the chamber of the sovereign, became
calm, respectful, and silent. They approached
the royal bed with a feeling of affectionate
deference, which restrained every intruder
from drawing back the curtains.

The queen herself performed this office.
She stood at the pillow of her son, beautiful in
features, of queenly grace in form and stature.
Pale, calm, and dignified as though she were
performing some ordinary court ceremonial,
she gathered back the folds of the velvet drapery, and revealed to the gaze of the people
their young sovereign in all the beauty of
youth, and apparently in profound slumber.

This living stream of men and women from
the streets of Paris continued to flow through
the chamber until three o'clock in the morn-

ing, entering at one door and passing out at its
opposite. Through this trying scene the queen
never faltered.

"Like a marble statue," writes Miss Pardoe,
"she retained her position, firm and motionless,
her majestic figure drawn haughtily to its full
height, and her magnificent arm resting in
broad relief upon the crimson draperies. And
still the boy-king, emulating the example of
his royal parent, remained immobile, with
closed eyes and steady breathing, as though
his rest had remained unbroken by the incur-
sion of his rebellious subjects. It was a singular and marked passage in the life of both
mother and son."*

In those days and at that court falsehood
was deemed an indispensable part of diplomacy. In the afternoon of the same day in
which the scene we have described occurred,
the queen assembled in her saloon in the palace the prominent magistrates of the city.
With firm voice and undaunted eye, she assured them that she had never entertained the
slightest idea of removing his majesty from
the city. She enjoined it upon them vigilantly to continue to guard the gates, that the pop-

* Louis XIV. and the Court of France, vol. i., page 351.

ulace might be convinced that no design of
escape was cherished. Her words were not
believed; her directions were obeyed. The
gates were rigidly closed. Thus the king was
a prisoner.

The apprehensions of the Fronde, that by
some stratagem the king might be removed,.
were so great that *Monsieur* dispatched a gentleman of his household every night to ascertain if the king were quietly in his bed. The
messenger, M. Desbuches, carried a nightly
greeting to the queen, with orders not to leave
the Palais Royal without seeing the young
sovereign. The excuse for this intrusion was,
that *Monsieur* could not, without this evidence,
satisfy the excited citizens that the king was
safe. This was a terrible humiliation to the
queen regent.

Cardinal Mazarin, having passed the night
at St. Germain, commenced traveling by slow
stages toward Havre. He was expecting every
hour to be joined by the queen regent and
other members of the royal household. He
was, however, overtaken by a courier, who announced to him what had transpired in Paris,
and that the escape of the royal family was
impossible. The cardinal thus found himself

really in exile, and earnest endeavors were made by the Fronde to induce the queen regent to secure a cardinal's hat for M. de Retz, and make him her prime minister. The last act of the queen regent was the issuing of a decree that Mazarin was banished forever from the kingdom.

Such was the posture of affairs when, on the 5th of September, 1651, the minority of the dauphin ceased. He now entered upon his fourteenth year, and, immature boy as he was, was declared to be the absolute monarch of France.

It was immediately announced to the Parliament by the grand master of ceremonies that on the seventh day of the month the king would hold his bed of justice. This name was given to the throne which the king took at extraordinary meetings of Parliament. The bed, or couch, was furnished with five cushions, and stood under a gorgeous canopy. Upon this couch the king extended himself, leaning upon the cushions.

The ceremony was attended with all the pomp which the wealth and taste of the empire could create. As, in the morning, the court left the Palais Royal, a band of trumpet-

ers led the van, causing the air to resound with
their bugle peals. These were followed by a
troop of light-horse, succeeded by two hundred
of the highest nobility of France, splendidly
mounted and in dazzling array. But it is vain
to attempt to describe the gorgeous procession
of dignitaries, mounted on tall war-horses, ca-
parisoned with housings embroidered with silver and gold, and accompanied by numerous
retainers. The attire of these attendants, from
the most haughty man of arms to the humblest
page, was as varied, picturesque, and glittering
as human ingenuity could devise.

The young king himself rode upon a magnificent cream-colored charger. He was a
beautiful boy, well formed and tall for his age.
Apparently deeply impressed with the grandeur of the occasion, he appeared calm and dignified to a degree which attracted the admiration of every beholder. As he sat gracefully
upon his horse, he appeared almost like a gold-
en statue, for his dress was so elaborately embroidered with gold that neither its material
or its color could be distinguished. His high-
mettled charger became frightened by the
shouts of "Long live the king" which burst so
enthusiastically from the lips of the crowd.

But Louis managed the animal with so much
skill and self-possession as to increase the admiration with which all seemed to regard him.
After attending mass, the young monarch took
his seat in the Parliament.   Here the boy of
thirteen, covering his head, while all the notabilities of France stood before him with heads
uncovered, repeated the following words:

"GENTLEMEN,—I have attended my Parliament in order to inform you that, according
to the law of my kingdom, I shall myself assume its government.   I trust that, by the
goodness of God, it will be with piety and justice.   My chancellor will inform you more
particularly of my intentions."

The chancellor then made a long address.
At its conclusion the queen mother rose and
said to her son:

"SIRE,—This is the ninth year in which, by
the last will of the deceased king, my much
honored lord, I have been intrusted with the
care of your education and the government of
the state.   God having by his will blessed my
endeavors, and preserved your person, which
is so precious to your subjects, now that the
law of the kingdom calls you to the rule of
this monarchy, I transfer to you, with great

satisfaction, the power which had been granted
me to govern. I trust that God will aid you
with his strength and wisdom, that your reign
may be prosperous."

To this the king replied, " I thank you, madame, for the care which it has pleased you to
take of my education and the administration
of my kingdom. I pray you to continue to
me your good advice, and desire that, after myself, you should be the head of my council."

The mother and the son embraced each other, and then resumed their conspicuous seats
on the platform. The king's brother, Philip,
duke of Anjou, next rose, and, sinking upon
his knee, took the oath of allegiance to his royal brother. He was followed in this act by
all the civil and ecclesiastical notabilities. The
royal procession returned to the gates of the
Palais Royal, greeted apparently by the unanimous acclamations of the people.

Thus a stripling, who had just completed his
thirteenth year, was accepted by the nobles
and by the populace as the absolute and un-
trammeled sovereign of France. He held in
his hands virtually, unrestrained by constitu-
tion or court, their liberties, their fortunes, and
their lives. It is often said that every nation

has as good a government as it deserves. In republican America, it seems incredible that a nation of twenty millions of people could have been guilty of the folly of surrendering themselves to the sway of a pert, weak, immature boy of thirteen years.

The young king, in those early years, was celebrated for his gallantry. A bevy of young beauties, from the most illustrious families in the realm, crowded his court. The matter of the marriage of the king was deemed of very great moment. According to the etiquette of the times, it was thought necessary that he should marry a lady of royal blood. It would have been esteemed a degradation for him to select the daughter of the highest noble, unless that noble were of the royal family. But these pretty girls were not unconscious of the power of their charms. The haughty Anne of Aus tria was constantly harassed by the flirtation in which the young king was continually engaging with these lovely maidens of the court.

Louis by nature, and still more by education, was egotistical, haughty, and overbearing. His brother Philip, on the contrary, was gentle, retiring, and effeminate. The young king wished to be the handsomest man of his court. the

most brilliant in wit, and the most fascinating
in the graces of social life. He was very jealous of any one of his companions who might
be regarded as his rival in personal beauty, or
in any intellectual or courtly accomplishment.
His mother encouraged this feeling. She desired that her son should stand in his court
without a peer.

Still Anne of Austria, in conjunction with
Cardinal Mazarin, had done what she could to
check the intellectual growth of her son.
Wishing to retain power as long as possible,
they had manifested no disposition to withdraw young Louis from the frivolities of childhood. His education had been grossly neglected. Though entirely familiar with the routine
of his devotional exercises, and all the punctilios of court etiquette, he was in mental culture
and general intelligence far below ordinary
school-boys of his age.

Though the king was nominally the absolute
ruler of France, still there were outside influences which exerted over him a great control.
There is no such thing as independent power.
All are creatures of circumstances. There
were two antagonistic forces brought to bear
upon the young king. Anne of Austria for

nine years had been regent. With the aid of
her prime minister, Cardinal Mazarin, she had
governed the realm. This power could not at
once and entirely pass from their hands to the
ignorant boy who was dallying with the little
beauties in the saloons of the Palais Royal.
Though Mazarin was in exile—an exile to
which the queen regent had been compelled to
assent — still he retained her confidence, and
an influence over her mind.

On the other hand, there was the Parliament, composed mainly of proud, haughty,
powerful nobles, the highest dignitaries of
Church and State. This body was under the
leadership of the coadjutor, M. de Retz. The
antagonism between the Parliament and the
court was by no means appeased. The great
conflict now rose, which continued through
months and years, between them, as to which
should obtain the control of the king. Impelled by the action of the Parliament, the
king had applied to the pope for a cardinal's
hat to be conferred upon M. de Retz. This
dignity attained would immeasurably increase
the power of the coadjutor.

In the mean time, Cardinal Mazarin, who
had fled to Spain, had re-entered France with

an army of six thousand men. Paris was thrown into a state of great agitation. Parliament was immediately assembled. The king sent them a message requesting the Parliament not to regard the movements of the cardinal with any anxiety, "since the intentions of his eminence were well known by the court." This, of course, increased rather than diminished the fears of the nobles. Notwithstanding the message of the king, a decree was immediately passed declaring the cardinal and his adherents disturbers of the public peace. The cardinal was outlawed. A sum equal to thirty thousand dollars, the proceeds of the sale of some property of the cardinal, was offered to any one who should deliver him either dead or alive. Unintimidated, Mazarin continued his march toward Paris, arriving at Poictiers at the end of January, one month after having re-entered France. The king, the queen regent, and the whole court advanced there to meet him. They received him with the greatest demonstrations of joy.

When the news reached the capital that Mazarin had thus triumphantly returned, Parliament and the populace were thrown into a state of great excitement. The Duke of Or-

1—5

leans was roused as never before. The hostile
demonstrations in Paris became so alarming,
that the royal family adopted the bold resolve
to return immediately to the capital. The
king commenced his march at the head of the
troops of the cardinal. When he reached
Blois, he tarried there for a couple of days to
concentrate his forces. Civil war was now inaugurated, though on rather a petty scale, between the hostile forces in various parts of the
kingdom. The Prince of Condé was the prominent leader of the Parliamentary troops.

The city of Blois is situated on the right
bank of the River Loire, about forty-five miles
below the city of Orleans, which is also on the
northern side of the same stream. At Blois,
the court learned to its consternation that the
Mazarin army had been attacked at Orleans
by the Prince de Condé and utterly routed,
with the loss of many prisoners, nearly three
thousand horses, and a large part of its ord-
nance stores. The royal party, which was at
this time in a state of great destitution, was
quite overwhelmed by the disaster. The queen
ordered all the equipages and baggage to be
transported to the south side of the Loire, and
the bridge to be broken down. At midnight,

in the midst of a scene of great terror and
confusion, this movement was accomplished.
As the morning dawned, the carriages, crowded with the ladies of the court, were seen on
the left bank of the stream, ready for flight.
The queen was, for the only time in her life,
so dejected as to seem utterly in despair.   She
feared that the triumph of the Fronde at Orleans would induce every city in the kingdom
to close its gates against the court.

The royal fugitives retreated to Montereau.
In the disorder of the flight they were exposed
to great privation.   Even the young king lost
several of his best horses.   Thence they proceeded to Corbeil, on the right bank of the
Seine, about twelve leagues from Versailles.
Here a scene occurred which is graphically
described by M. Laporte, an eye-witness, who
was a prominent attendant of his majesty.

"The king," writes Laporte, "insisted that
*Monsieur** should sleep in his room, which
was so small that but one person could pass at
a time.   In the morning, as they lay awake,

* As Louis XIV. was now king, his brother Philip, eleven
years of age, according to usage, took the title of *Monsieur.*
The title for a time adhered still to the Duke of Orleans,
brother of Louis XIII.

the king inadvertently spat upon the bed of
Monsieur, who immediately spat upon the
king's bed in return.   Thereupon Louis, get-
ting angry, spat in his brother's face.   When
they could spit no longer, they proceeded to
drag each other's sheets upon the floor, after
which they prepared to fight.   During this
quarrel I did what I could to restrain the king.
As I could not succeed, I sent for M. de Villeroi, who re-established peace.   *Monsieur* lost
his temper sooner than the king, but the king
was much more difficult to appease."

It is very evident that aristocratic titles, and
all the formalities of court etiquette, do not
change the nature of boyhood.   Though one
of these little belligerents bore the title of
Louis XIV., king of France, and the other was
called Monsieur, the duke of Anjou, they were
in character like all other ungoverned and un-
governable boys.

The court, not venturing to enter Paris, pursued its way by a circuitous route to St. Germain, leaving the city on the left.   Here an
additional gloom was cast over their spirits by
the intelligence of very decided acts of hostility manifested against them by the inhabitants
of the metropolis.   The court was in a state

of great embarrassment, without any money,
and without possibility of obtaining stores from
the capital. It was supposed that Cardinal
Mazarin, noted for his selfishness, had taken
good care of himself. But he declared that
he was as poor as the meanest soldier in the
ranks.

While at St. Germain, there was another petty conflict between the Parliamentary forces
and those of the court in the vicinity of
Etampes, about forty miles from Versailles.
The Fronde was routed with loss. The glad
tidings was brought by a courier at night to St.
Germain. The news was too good to be kept
till morning. M. Villeroi, to whom it was at
first communicated, hastened to the chamber
of the king and the Duke of Anjou, to awake
them from sleep and inform them of the victory. They both, Laporte informs us, sprang
from their beds, and rushed, in their slippers,
night-caps, and dressing-gowns, to the chamber
of the cardinal, whom they awakened with the
joyful tidings. He hurried in his turn with
them, and in the same unsophisticated costume,
to the chamber of the queen, to announce the
intelligence to her.

The destitution of Louis XIV. while at St.

Germain was such that he borrowed one hundred and ten francs from Moreau, one of his valets, for some replenishment of his wardrobe. Subsequently the valet, learning that the king had obtained possession of one hundred *louis d'or*, applied for payment of the debt; but the king had already expended the coin.

The routed troops of Condé took refuge within the walls of Etampes. The court, in its elation, immediately proceeded from St. Germain to the scene of conflict, to take part in the siege. This was the first serious campaign of the young king. As, attended by his suite, he examined the works, he was at one time under fire, and several bullets passed near him. Still young as he was, he had sufficient regard for his reputation and control over himself not to manifest the slightest fear.

The scenes of war which here presented themselves to the young monarch were painful in the extreme. He was every where surrounded by sick and dying soldiers. But he had no money with which to relieve their misery, and when finally the city of Etampes was taken, the spectacle of starvation, woe, and death was more awful than words can express.

As the king was entering the city, he passed

a group lying upon the ground, consisting of
a mother and three children, huddled closely
together. The mother had died of starvation.
Two of the skeleton children were also dead
by her side, and the third, a babe, was strain-
ing at the exhausted breast, which could no
longer afford it any nourishment.

The Prince de Condé retreated to Paris with
about three thousand men. The royal troops,
eight thousand in number, pursued. Each party gathered re-enforcements, so that the Prince
de Condé, with about five thousand men, held
at bay the royal troops, then numbering about
ten thousand. The citizens, as we have mentioned, were in sympathy with the Parliament.
They hated Cardinal Mazarin, and with good
reason regarded the king as a prisoner in his
hands. The king also detested Mazarin per-
sonally, while the force of circumstances compelled him to regard the cardinal as the advocate of the royal cause.

A very severe battle was fought between
the two parties in the Faubourg St. Antoine.
The ranks of the Fronde, shattered by over-
powering numbers, were, in a disordered retreat, hotly pursued by their foes under Marshal Turenne. The carnage was dreadful.

Suddenly the cannon of the Bastile flamed out
in rapid succession, hurling their deadly shot
through the compact masses of the Royalists.
They recoiled and fled in confusion. Paris
was in the hands of the Fronde. The populace surged through the streets, shouting "Long
live the king! Death to Mazarin!"

The cardinal, taking the king with him, retired to St. Denis. Turenne re-collected his
scattered forces at Pontoise, about twenty miles
north from Versailles. The cardinal, with the
king, took refuge at that place in the centre
of Turenne's army. Here the king issued an
ordinance, transferring the Parliament from
Paris to Pontoise; but the Parliament replied
"that they could not obey the royal command
so long as Cardinal Mazarin, whom they had
outlawed, remained in France." They also issued an ordinance of their own, forbidding any
member of the Parliament to leave Paris. The
king, we know not under what influences, ac-
quiesced in both of these decrees. This led
the cardinal immediately to tender his resigna-
tion and retire. This important step changed
the whole aspect of affairs. After the removal
of the cardinal, all opposition to the court became rebellion against the king, to whom the
Fronde professed entire allegiance.

THE TUILERIES.

Parliament immediately issued a decree, thanking the king for banishing the cardinal, and imploring him to return to his good city of Paris. After some negotiation the king acceded to their wishes, and on the 17th of October arrived at St. Germain. Here a numerous civic guard and deputation hastened to greet him, and to conduct him to the metropolis. On the 20th he proceeded to Ruel, where he passed the night.

The king decided to enter the city at the head of his army. In order to render the scene more imposing, it was to take place at night, by the light of thousands of torches. The spectacle was such as Paris had rarely witnessed. The fickle people, ever ready to vibrate between the cry of hosanna and crucify, pealed forth their most enthusiastic rejoicings. The triumphant boy-king took possession of the Tuileries. Cardinal de Retz, who had now gained his long-coveted ecclesiastical distinction, hastened to congratulate the king and his mother upon their return to the city, from which they had so long been banished. The Duke of Orleans, chagrined and humiliated, retired to Blois.

The king soon held what was called a bed

of justice, in which, instead of granting a general amnesty, he denounced the princes Condé
and Conti, and other of the prominent leaders
of the Fronde, as traitors to their king, to be
punished by death. These doomed ones were
nobles of high rank, vast wealth, with thousands of retainers. Many throughout the kingdom were in sympathy with them. They
would not die without a struggle. Hence the
war, which had hitherto raged between Mazarin and the Fronde, was renewed between the
king and the Fronde. All over the provinces
the hostile forces were rallying themselves for
the conflict.

It was necessary that the Parliament should
register this decree of the king. It did so, but
Cardinal de Retz refused to give his vote. He
very respectfully declared to the king that he,
having been on friendly terms and in co-operation with the Prince de Condé, it would be
neither courteous nor just for him to vote his
condemnation.

This enraged both the king and his mother.
They said it proved that he was in sympathy
with their enemies. The court did not venture
at once to strike down one so formidable. A
mission was assigned the cardinal at Rome, to

remove him from the country. He refused to
accept it. The boy-king was growing reckless,
passionate, self-willed. He began to feel the
power that was in his hand. The cardinal
was warned of his danger. He smiled, and
said " that, sustained by his ecclesiastical rank,
he had nothing to fear."

The court issued an order for the arrest of
the cardinal. It was placed in the hands of
Pradelle for execution. But the king was told
that the cardinal would never suffer himself
to be arrested without resistance; that, to se
cure his seizure, it might be necessary to take
his life. The king seized a pen and wrote at
the bottom of the order,

" I have commanded Pradelle to execute the
present order on the person of De Retz, and
even to arrest him, dead or alive, in the event
of resistance on his part.   Louis."

It was deemed very important to arrest the
cardinal, if possible, without exciting a popular
tumult. The palace of the cardinal was well
guarded. He never went out without a numerous retinue. Should the populace of Paris
see him endangered, they would spring to his
rescue.

At length De Retz was earnestly invited to

78   LOUIS XIV.   [1652.

Treachery of Anne of Austria.   Arrest of De Retz.

visit the queen at the Louvre, in token that he
was not hostile to the court. It was one of the
most dishonorable of stratagems. The cardinal was caught in the trap. As he was entering the antechamber of the queen upon this
visit of friendship, all unsuspicious of treachery, the captain of the guard, who had been
stationed there for the purpose with several
gendarmes, seized him, hurried him through
the great gallery of the Louvre, and down the
stairs to the door. Here a royal carriage was
awaiting him. He was thurst into the carriage, and five or six officers took seats by his
side. To guard against any possibility of rescue, a numerous military escort was at hand.
The horses were driven rapidly through the
streets, and out through the Porte St. Antoine.

At nine o'clock the cardinal found himself
a prisoner at the castle of Vincennes. The
apartment assigned him was cold and dreary,
without furniture and without a bed. Here
the prisoner remained a fortnight, in the middle of December, with no fire.

The arrest of the cardinal created a great
sensation throughout Paris. But the chateau
was too strong, and too vigilantly guarded by
the royal troops, to encourage any attempt at
a rescue.

THE CASTLE OF VINCENNES.

In the mean time, Mazarin had placed himself at the head of the royal troops in one of the provinces, where he gained several unimportant victories over the bands of the Fronde. These successes were trumpeted abroad as great achievements, so as to invest the cardinal with the renown of a great conqueror. Mazarin was well aware of the influence of military glory upon the populace in Paris. The king also began to feel the need of his dominant mind. He was invited to return to Paris. Louis himself rode out six miles beyond the walls to receive him. The cardinal entered the city in triumph, in the same carriage with his sovereign, and seated by his side. All the old idols were forgotten, and the once detested Mazarin was received as though he were an angel from heaven. Bonfires and illuminations blazed through the streets; the whole city resounded with demonstrations of rejoicing. Thus terminated the year 1652.

The first care of Cardinal Mazarin, after his return to Paris, was to restore the finances, which were in a deplorable condition. Louis was fond of pleasure. It was one great object of the cardinal to gratify him in this respect, in every possible way. Notwithstanding the

1—6

penury of the court, the cardinal contrived to supply the king with money. Thus, during the winter, the royal palaces resounded with festivity and dissipation. The young king became very fond of private theatricals, in which he, his brother Philip, and the young ladies of the court took prominent parts. Louis often appeared upon the stage in the character of a ballet-dancer. He was proud of the grace with which he could perform the most difficult pirouettes. He had plays written, with parts expressly composed for his aristocratic troop.

The scene of these masqueradings was the theatre of the Hotel du Petit Bourbon, which was contiguous to the Louvre. When royalty plays and courtiers fill pit and gallery, applause is without stint. The boy-king was much elated with his theatric triumphs. The queen and Cardinal Mazarin were well pleased to see the king expending his energies in that direction.

These entertainments cost money, which Mazarin was greatly embarrassed in obtaining. The hour was approaching for the coronation of Louis. The pageant would require large sums of money to invest the occasion with the desirable splendor. But gold was not all that was wanted. Rank, brilliance, beauty were requisite suitably to impress the masses of the people. But the civil war had robbed the court of many of its most attractive ornaments.

Monsieur, the duke of Orleans, was sullenly residing at Blois. Here he held a somewhat rival court to the king. He refused to attend the coronation unless certain concessions were granted, to which Mazarin could not give his consent. Mademoiselle, the duchess of Montpensier, daughter of Monsieur by his first wife, a young lady of wonderful heroism and attractions, who possessed an enormous property in her own right, and who was surrounded by a brilliant court of her own, could not consistently share in festivities at which her father refused to appear.

The Prince of Condé, one of the highest nobles of the realm, and who had many adherents of the most illustrious rank, was in arms against his king at the head of the Spanish forces, and sentence of death had been pronounced upon him.

Cardinal de Retz was a prisoner at Vincennes. His numerous followers in Church and State refused to sanction by their presence any movements of a court thus persecuting their beloved cardinal.

It was thus impossible to invest the coronation with the splendor which the occasion seemed to demand.

The coronation took place, however, at Rheims. Cardinal Mazarin exerted all his ingenuity to render the pageant imposing; but the absence of so many of the most illustrious of the realm cast an atmosphere of gloom around the ceremonies.

France was at the time at war with Spain. The Fronde co-operated with the Spanish troops in the civil war. Immediately after the coronation, the king, then sixteen years of age, left Rheims to place himself at the head of the army. He repaired to Stenay, on the Meuse, in the extreme northeastern frontier of France. This ancient city, protected by strong fortifications, was held by Condé. The royal troops were besieging it. The poverty of the treasury was such that Mazarin could not furnish Louis even with the luxury of a carriage. He traveled on horseback. He had no table of his own, but shared in that of the Marquis de Fabert, the general in command.

It seems difficult to account for the fact that the young king was permitted to enter the trenches, and to engage in skirmishes,

Defeat of Condé.

where he was so exposed to the fire of the enemy that the wounded and the dead were continually falling around him. He displayed
much courage on these occasions.

The Prince of Condé left a garrison in one
of the strong fortresses, and marched with the
main body of his troops to Arras. The movements of the two petty armies, their skirmishes
and battles, are no longer of any interest. The
battles were fought and the victories gained
by the direction of the generals Turenne and
Fabert. Though the boy-king displayed in-
trepidity which secured for him the respect of
the soldiers, he could exert but little influence
either in council or on the field. Both Stenay
and Arras were soon taken. The army of the
Prince of Condé was driven from all its posi-
tions.

The king returned to Paris to enjoy the grat-
ulation of the populace, and to offer public
thanksgiving in the cathedral of Notre Dame.

CHAPTER III.

MATRIMONIAL PROJECTS.

"THERE is nothing so successful as success." The young king returned to Paris
from his coronation and his brief campaign a
hero and a conqueror. The courage he had
displayed won universal admiration. The ex-
citable populace were half frenzied with enthusiasm. The city resounded with shouts of glad-
ness, and the streets were resplendent with the
display of gorgeous pageants.

The few nobles who still rallied around the
court endeavored to compensate by the magnificence of their equipages, the elegance of
their attire, and the splendor of their festivities, for their diminished numbers. There
were balls and tournaments, where the dress
and customs of the by-gone ages of chivalry
were revived. Ladies of illustrious birth, glittering in jewels, and proud in conscious beauty, contributed to the gorgeousness of the spectacle. Still, in the midst of all this splendor,
the impoverished court was greatly embarrassed by straitened circumstances.

Cardinal Mazarin, eager to retain his hold upon the king, did every thing he could to gratify the love of pleasure which his royal master developed, and strove to multiply seductive amusements to engross his time and thoughts.

But a few days after Cardinal de Retz had been conducted a prisoner to Vincennes, his uncle, the Archbishop of Paris, died. The cardinal could legally claim the succession. The metropolitan clergy, who had been almost roused to rebellion by his arrest, were now still more deeply moved, since he had become their archbishop. They regarded his captivity as political martyrdom, and their murmurs were deep and prolonged. The pope also addressed several letters to the court, soliciting the liberation of his cardinal. The excitement daily increased. Nearly all the pulpits more or less openly denounced his captivity. At length a pamphlet appeared urging the clergy to close all their churches till their archbishop should be released.

Mazarin was frightened. He sent an envoy to the captive cardinal presenting terms of compromise. We have not space to describe the diplomacy which ensued, but the conference was unavailing. The cardinal was soon after removed, under an escort of dragoons, to the fortress of Nantes. From this place he almost miraculously escaped to his own territory of Retz, where he was regarded as sovereign, and where he was surrounded by retainers who, in impregnable castles, would fight to the death for their lord. These scenes took place early in the summer of 1653.

In the mean time, the young king was amusing himself in his various palaces with the many beautiful young ladies who embellished his court. Like other lads of fifteen, he was in the habit of falling in love with one and another, though the transient passion did not seem very deeply to affect his heart. Some of these maidens were exceedingly beautiful. In others, vivacity and intellectual brilliance quite eclipsed the charms of the highest physical loveliness.

Anne of Austria, forgetting that the all-dominant passion of love had led her to regret that she was the wife of the king, that she might marry the Duke of Buckingham, did not deem it possible that her son could stoop so low as to marry any one who was not of royal blood. She therefore regarded without much uneasiness his desperate flirtations, while she was scanning the courts of Europe in search of an alliance which would add to the power and the renown of her son.

One of the nieces of Cardinal Mazarin, an Italian girl by the name of Olympia Mancini, was among the first to whom the boy-king of fifteen became specially attached. Olympia was very beautiful, and her personal fascinations were rivaled by her mental brilliance, wit, and tact. She was by nature and education a thorough coquette, amiable and endearing to an unusual degree. She had a sister a little older than herself, who was also extremely beautiful, who had recently become the Duchess of Mercœur. Etiquette required that in the balls which the king attended every evening he should recognize the rank of the duchess by leading her out first in the dance. After this, he devoted himself exclusively, for the remainder of the evening, to Olympia.

It will be remembered that Henrietta, the widowed queen of Charles II., who was daughter of Henry IV. and sister of Louis XIII., was then residing in France. She had no pecuniary means of her own, and, chagrined and humiliated, was a pensioner upon the bounty

of the impoverished French court. Henrietta
had with her a very pretty daughter, eleven
years of age. Being the granddaughter of
Henry IV. and daughter of Charles II., she
was entitled, through the purity of her royal
blood, to the highest consideration in the etiquette of the court. But the mother and the
daughter, from their poverty and their misfortunes, were precluded from any general partic-
ipation in the festivities of the palace.

The queen, Anne of Austria, on one occasion, gave a private ball in honor of these unfortunate guests in her own apartments. None
were invited but a few of her most intimate
friends. Henrietta attended with her daughter, who bore her mother's name. There are
few situations more painful than that of poor
relatives visiting their more prosperous friends,
who in charity condescend to pay them some
little attention. The young Henrietta was a
fragile and timid girl, who keenly felt the embarrassment of her situation. As, with her
face suffused with blushes, and her eyes moist-
ened with the conflicting emotions of joyousness and fear, she entered the brilliant saloon
of Anne of Austria, crowded with those below
her in rank, but above her in prosperity and

all worldly aggrandizement, she was received coldly, with no marks of sympathy or attention. As the music summoned the dancers to the floor, the king, neglecting his young and royal cousin, advanced, according to his custom, to the Duchess of Mercœur, to lead her out. The queen, shocked at so gross a breach of etiquette, and even of kindly feeling, rose from her seat, and, advancing, withdrew the hand of the duchess from her son, and said to him, in a low voice, "You should dance first with the English princess." The boy-king sulkily replied, "I am not fond of little girls." Both Henrietta and her daughter overheard this uncourteous and cruel remark.

Henrietta, the mother, hastened to the queen, and entreated her not to attempt to constrain the wishes of his majesty. It was an exceedingly awkward position for all the parties. The spirit of Anne of Austria was aroused. Resuming her maternal authority, she declared that if her niece, the Princess of England, were to remain a spectator at the ball, her son should do the same. Thus constrained, Louis very ungraciously led out Henrietta upon the floor. The young princess, tender in years, sensitive through sorrow, wounded and heart-crushed, danced with tears streaming down her cheeks.

Upon the departure of the guests, the mother and the son had their first serious quarrel. Anne rebuked Louis severely for his shameful conduct. The king rebelled. Haughtily facing his mother, he said, " I have long enough been guided by your leading-strings. I shall submit to it no longer." It was a final declaration of independence. Though there were tears shed on both sides, and the queen made strenuous efforts at conciliation, she felt, and justly felt, that the control of her son had passed from her forever. It was a crisis in the life of the king. From that hour he seemed disposed on all occasions to assert his manhood.

A remarkable indication of this soon occurred. It was customary, when the king, through his ministers, issued any decrees, that they should be registered by the Parliament, to give them full authority. Some very oppressive decrees had been issued to raise funds for the court. It was deemed very important that they should be registered. The king in person attended Parliament, that the influence of his presence might carry the measure. No one dared to oppose in the presence of the king.

Louis had now established his summer residence at the castle of Vincennes. Arrangements had been made for a magnificent hunt in the forest the next day, to be attended by all the ladies and gentlemen of the court. The king, after leaving the Parliament, returned to Vincennes, which is about three miles from Paris. He had scarcely arrived at the castle when he received information that, immediately upon his leaving the Parliament, a motion had been made to reconsider the approval of the decrees.

The king dispatched a courier ordering the Chamber to reassemble the next morning. The pleasure-loving courtiers were dismayed by this order, as they thought it would interfere with the hunt. But the king assured them that business should not be allowed to interfere with his pleasures.

At half past nine o'clock the next morning the king entered the chamber of deputies in his hunting-dress. It consisted of a scarlet coat, a gray beaver hat, and high military boots. He was followed by a large retinue of the nobles of his court in a similar costume.

"In this unusual attire," writes the Marquis de Montglat, "the king heard mass, took his

place with the accustomed ceremonies, and,
with a whip in his hand, declared to the Parliament that in future it was his will that his
edicts should be registered, and not discussed.
He threatened them that, should the contrary
occur, he would return and enforce obedience."

How potent must have been the circumstances which the feudalism of ages had created.
These assembled nobles yielded without a
murmur to this insolence from a boy of eighteen. Parliament had ventured to try its
strength against Cardinal Mazarin, but did not
dare to disobey its king.

Soon after this, Louis, having learned that
Turenne had gained some important victories
over the Fronde, decided to join the army to
witness the siege of the city of Condé and of
St. Quilain. Both of these places soon fell
into the hands of the Royalist troops. The
king had looked on. Rapidly he returned to
Paris to enjoy almost a Roman triumph for
his great achievement.

As one of the festivities of the city, the king
arranged a tournament in honor of his avowed
lady-love, Olympia Mancini. She occupied a
conspicuous seat among the ladies of the court,
her lovely person decorated with a dress of ex-

quisite taste and beauty. The king was prominent in his attire among all the knights assembled to contest the palm of chivalry. He was dressed in robes of brilliant scarlet. A white scarf encircled his waist, and snow-white plumes waved gracefully from his hat.

The scene was as gorgeous as the wealth and decorative art of the court could create. There were retainers surrounding the high lords, and heralds, and pages, and trumpeters, all arrayed in the most picturesque costume. No one could be so discourteous or impolitic as to vanquish the king. He consequently bore away all the laurels. This magnificent tournament gave the name of " The Carousal" to the space where it was held, between the Louvre and the Tuileries.

Early in the summer the court removed to Compiègne, to spend the season in rural amusements there. Christina, the young queen of Sweden, who had just abdicated the throne, and whose eccentricities had attracted the attention of Europe, came to the frontiers of France with an imposing retinue, and, announcing her arrival, awaited the invitation of the king to visit his court. She was one of the most extraordinary personages of that or any

age. Good looking, "strong minded" to the
highest degree, masculine in dress and address,
always self-possessed, absolutely fearing nothing, proud, haughty, speaking fluently eight
languages, familiar with art, and a consummate
intriguante, she excited astonishment and a
certain degree of admiration wherever she appeared.

The curiosity of Louis was so greatly excited
and so freely expressed to see this extraordinary personage as to arouse the jealousy of
Olympia. The king perceived this. It is one
of the most detestable traits in our fallen nature that one can take pleasure in making another unhappy. The unamiable king amused
himself in torturing the feelings of Olympia.

Christina proceeded at first to Paris. Here
she was received with the greatest honor.
For a distance of nearly six miles from the
Louvre the streets were lined with armed citizens, who greeted her with almost unintermitted applause. The crowd was so great that,
though she reached the suburbs of Paris at two
o'clock in the afternoon, she did not alight at
the Louvre until nine o'clock in the evening.
This eccentric princess was then thirty years
of age, and, though youthful in appearance, in

PALACE OF CHANTILLY.

dress and manners she affected the Amazon. She had great powers of pleasing, and her wit, her entire self-reliance, and extensive information, enabled her to render herself very attractive whenever she wished to do so.

After spending a few days in Paris, she proceeded to Compiègne to visit the king and queen. Louis and his brother, with Mazarin and a crowd of courtiers, rode out as far as Chantilly, a distance of nearly twenty miles, to meet her. Christina also traveled in state, accompanied by an imposing retinue. Here there was, at that time, one of the largest and finest structures in France. The castle belonged to the family of Condé. The opposite cut presents it to the reader as it then appeared.

The king and his brother, from some freak, presented themselves to her at first *incognito*. They were introduced by Mazarin as two of the most nobly born gentlemen in France. Christina smiled, and promptly replied,

" Yes, I have no doubt of it, since their birthright is a crown."

She had seen their portraits in the Louvre the day before, and immediately recognized them.

Christina was to be honored with quite a triumphal entrance to Compiègne. The king

accordingly returned to Compiègne, and the
next day, with the whole court in carriages,
rode out a few leagues to a very splendid mansion belonging to one of the nobles at Fayet.
It was a lovely day, warm and cloudless.
Anne of Austria decided to receive her illustrious guest upon the spacious terrace. There
she assembled her numerous court, resplendent
with gorgeous dresses, and blazing with diamonds. Soon the carriage of the Swedish
queen drove up, with the loud clatter of out-
riders and the flourish of trumpets. Cardinal
Mazarin and the Duke de Guise assisted her
to alight. As she ascended the terrace the
queen advanced to meet her.

Though Anne was at first struck with amaze-
ment at the ludicrous appearance of the attire
of Christina, she was immediately fascinated
by her conversational tact and brilliance.
Some allusion having been made to the portrait of the king in the Louvre, the queen held
out her arm to show a still more faithful miniature in the clasp of her bracelet. Anne of
Austria had a very beautiful arm, and was
very proud of it. Christina, instead of looking
at the bracelet, surveyed the undraped arm
and hand with admiration.

"How beautiful! how beautiful!" she exclaimed. "Never did I see an arm and hand
of such lovely hue and such exquisite symmetry. I would willingly have made the journey
from Rome to Paris to see this arm."

The queen's heart was won, Christina knew
it. The next achievement was to win the king.

Christina was apparently as familiar with
the French court, and all the intrigues there,
from the information which she had obtained,
as if she had always been a resident at that
court. She immediately turned with very
marked attention to Olympia Mancini, and
seemed dazzled by her beauty. The heart of
the boy-king was won in seeing his own good
taste thus highly appreciated and sanctioned.
Having thus secured the queen and the king,
Christina was well aware that she had captiva-
ted the whole court.

An elegant collation was prepared. The
plump little queen ate like a hungry dragoon.
The royal cortége, enveloping the Swedish
princess, returned to the palace of Compiègne.
Several days were spent at Compiègne, during
which she astonished every one by the remarkable self-poise of her character, her varied information, and the versatility of her talents.

She conversed upon theology with the ecclesiastics, upon politics with the ministers, upon
all branches of science and art with philoso-
phers and the *virtuosi,* and eclipsed the most
brilliant of the courtiers in the small-talk of
gallantry.

She attended the theatre with the queen.
During the tragedy she wept like a child,
heartily and unaffectedly. During the farce,
which was one of those coarse and pungent
compositions by the poet Scarron, which would
now be scarcely tolerated, her shouts of laughter echoed through the theatre. She astonished the court by clapping her hands and throwing her feet upon the top of the royal box, like
a rowdy in a smoking-room.

From Compiègne, Christina, by invitation,
went to Fontainebleau to visit Mademoiselle de
Montpensier. The piquant pen of Mademoiselle has described this interview. Some al-
lowance must perhaps be made for the vein of
satire which pervaded nearly all the utterances
of this haughty princess. The dress of Christina consisted of a skirt of gray silk, trimmed
with gold and silver lace, with a bodice of gold-
colored camlet trimmed like the skirt. She
wore a kerchief of Genoa point about her neck,

VIEW OF FONTAINEBLEAU.

fastened with a knot of white ribbon.   A light
wig concealed her natural hair.   Her hat was
profusely decorated with white plumes.   She
looked, upon the whole, Mademoiselle thought,
like a handsome boy.

Mademoiselle, accustomed to the rigid propriety of the French court, was not a little surprised to hear Christina, during the comedy,
interlard her conversation with hearty oaths,
with all the volubility of an old guardsman.
She flung about her legs in the most astonish-
ing manner, throwing them over the arms of
her chair, and placing herself in attitudes quite
unprecedented in Parisian circles.

Soon after this, this Amazonian princess returned by a circuitous route to her Northern
home.   Before taking leave of her, it may be
well to remark that subsequently Christina
made a second visit to France uninvited—not
only uninvited, but very unwelcome.   She
took possession of the palace of Fontainebleau
with her attendants, where with cold courtesy
she was tolerated.   In a freak of passion, she
accused her grand equerry, M. Monaldeschi, of
high treason, and actually put him to death.
So high-handed an outrage, even in those days
of feudal barbarism, excited throughout France

a universal feeling of disgust and indignation. The sentiment was so strong and general that the king deemed it necessary to send her a letter through his minister, Mazarin, expressive of his extreme displeasure.

Christina, much exasperated, sent a reply containing the following expressions:

"MR. MAZARIN,—Those who acquainted you with the details regarding Monaldeschi, my equerry, were very ill informed. Your proceeding ought not, however, to astonish me, silly as it is. But I should never have believed that either you or your haughty young master would have dared to exhibit the least resentment toward me. Learn all of you, valets and masters, little and great, that it was my pleasure to act as I did; that I need not, and I will not account for my actions to any one in the world, and particularly to bullies of your description. I wish you to know, and to say to all who will hear it, that Christina cares very little about your court, and still less about yourself; and that, in order to revenge my wrongs, I do not require to have recourse to your formidable power. Believe me, therefore, Jules,* you had better conduct yourself

* Jules, the Christian name of Mazarin.

in a manner to deserve my favor, which you can not study too much to secure. God preserve you from ever risking the least indiscreet remark upon my person. Although at the end of the earth, I shall be informed of your plots. I have friends and courtiers in my service who are as clever and far-sighted as yours, although they are not so well paid. CHRISTINA."

Soon after this her Swedish majesty disappeared from France, to the great relief of the court, and was seen there no more.

Olympia Mancini had ever increasing evidence that the love of the king for her was but a frivolous and heartless passion. The Count de Soissons, of Savoy, a young prince who had just become the head of his house, visited the court of Louis XIV. The marvelous beauty of Olympia, at first glance, won his heart. He was young, handsome, chivalric, high-born, and was just entering upon a magnificent inheritance. Olympia had recently lost by death a mother whom she greatly revered, and a beloved sister. She was overwhelmed with grief. The entire want of sympathy manifested by the king shocked her. He thought of nothing but his own personal pleasure. Regardless of the grief of Olympia, he exhibited himself, evening after evening, in court theatricals, emulating the agility of an opera-dancer, and attired in spangled robes.

Wounded and irritated by such conduct, Olympia accepted the proffered hand of the Count de Soissons, who was grandson of Charles V. The marriage was attended with great splendor at the palace of the Louvre. All the court was present. The king himself seemed not at all discomposed that another should marry the beautiful maiden whom he had professed so ardently to love. Indeed, he was already beginning to transfer his attentions to Mademoiselle d'Argencourt, a queenly beauty of the high family of Conti. Her figure was perfect, her manners were courtly in the highest degree, and all who approached her were charmed with her conversational vivacity and tact.

But Mademoiselle's affections were already engaged, and, being fully aware that the king flitted from beauty to beauty, like the butterfly from flower to flower, she very frankly intimated to the king that she could not receive his attentions. Louis was heart-broken; for such fragile hearts are easily broken and as easily repaired. He hastened to his mother, and told her that he must leave Paris to conquer his passion. The love-sick monarch retired to Vincennes, spent ten days there, and returned quite cured.

The marriage of Olympia, as we have mentioned, was celebrated with very great brilliance. The ambitious cardinal, in heart disappointed that he had not been able to confer the hand of Olympia on the king, was increasingly desirous of investing the members of his family with all possible eclât. He had imported for the occasion the principal members of the Pope's choir. These wonderful vocalists from the Sistine Chapel astonished the French court with melody and harmony such as had never been heard in the Louvre before.

Olympia had a younger sister, Mary, fifteen years of age. She had come from her school in a convent to witness the marriage festivities. The music and the impressive scene affected the artless child deeply, and her tears flowed freely. The king, surrounded by the brilliant beauties of his court, accidentally caught sight of this child. Though not beautiful, there was something in her unaffected attitude, her tears, her entire absorption in the scene, which arrested his attention.

Mary had early developed so bold, independent, and self-reliant a spirit as to induce her father, on his death-bed, to entreat Madame de Mancini to compel her to take the veil. In compliance with this injunction, Mary had been placed in a convent until she should attain the fitting age to assume the irrevocable vows. Thus trained in seclusion, and with no ambitious aspirations, she had acquired a character of perfect simplicity, and her countenance bore an expression of intelligence and sensibility far more attractive than ordinary beauty. A contemporaneous writer says,

"Her movements, her manners, and all the bearing of her person were the result of a nature guided by grace. Her look was tender, the accents of her voice were enchanting. Her genius was great, substantial, and extensive, and capable of the grandest conceptions. She wrote both good prose and pleasing poetry; and Mary Mancini, who shone in a courtly letter, was equally capable of producing a political or state dispatch. She would not have been unworthy of the throne if among us great merit had been entitled to obtain it."

The king inquired her name. Upon learning that she was a niece of the cardinal, and a sister of Olympia, he desired that she might be presented to him.

Mary was an enthusiast. The young king was very handsome, very courtly, and a perfect master of all the phrases of gallantry. Mary fell in love with him, without knowing it, at first sight. It was not the *monarch* which had won her, but the *man*, of exquisitely symmetrical proportions, so princely in his bearing, so fascinating in his address. The young school-girl returned to her convent with the image of the king indelibly engraven on her heart. The few words which passed between them interested the king, for every word she said bore the impress of her genius. Ere long she was added to the ladies of the queen's household.

The king, having closed his flirtation with Mademoiselle d'Argencourt, found himself almost insensibly drawn to Mary Mancini. Though there were many in his court more beautiful in person, there were none who could rival her in intellect and wit. Though naturally timid, her reserve disappeared when in his presence. Though ever approaching him with the utmost possible deference and respect, she conversed with him with a frankness to which he was entirely unaccustomed, and

which, at the same time, surprised and charmed him.

His vanity was gratified with the almost religious devotion with which she unaffectedly
regarded her sovereign, while at the same time
she addressed him with a bold simplicity of
utterance which astounded the courtiers and
enthralled the king. He was amazed and bewildered by the grandeur of a character such
as he had never encountered before. She re-
proved him for his faults, instructed him in his
ignorance, conversed with him upon themes
beyond the ordinary range of his intellect, and
endeavored to enkindle within him noble im-
pulses and a lofty ambition. The king found
himself quite unable to compete with her
strength of intellect. His weaker nature became more and more subject to one endowed
with gifts far superior to his own. In every
hour of perplexity, in every serious moment,
when the better nature of the king gained a
transient ascendency, he turned from the frivolity of the gay and thoughtless beings flut-
tering around him to Mary Mancini for guidance and strength.

The ambition of Cardinal Mazarin was again
excited with the hope that he might yet place

a niece upon the throne of France. But there
was no end to the intrigues of ambitious aspi-
rants, directly or indirectly, for the hand of the
young king. Mademoiselle de Montpensier
had enormous wealth, was of high birth, and
was endowed with marvelous force of character. She had long aspired to share the throne
with her young cousin. When it was evident
that this plan had failed, the Duke of Orleans
brought forward a younger daughter by a second wife. But Mazarin succeeded in thwart-
ing this arrangement. The Princess Henrietta
of England, whom the young king had treated
so cruelly at the ball, was urged upon him.
She was lovely in person, amiable in character,
but in poverty and exile. Cromwell was in
the plenitude of his power. There was no
probability that her family would be restored
to the throne. The king turned coldly from
her.

Portugal was then one of the most wealthy
and powerful courts of Europe. The Queen of
Portugal was exceedingly anxious to unite her
daughter with the King of France. Through
her embassadors she endeavored to effect an
alliance. A portrait of the princess was sent
to Louis. It was very beautiful. The king

1—8

made private inquiries. She was very plain.
This settled the question. The Portuguese
princess was thought of no more.

The King of Spain had a very beautiful
daughter, Maria Theresa. The Spanish monarchy then, perhaps, stood second to none other on the globe. Spain and France were engaged in petty and vexatious hostilities. A
matrimonial alliance would secure friendship.
The matter was much talked of. The proud
queen-mother, Anne of Austria, was very solic-
itous to secure that alliance, as it would gratify her highest ambition. Mazarin professed
warmly to favor it. He probably saw insuperable obstacles in the way, but hoped, by co-
operating cordially with the wishes of the
queen, to be able finally to secure the marriage
of the king with Mary Mancini.

Maria Theresa was heiress to the throne of
Spain. Should she marry Louis XIV., it would
be necessary for her to leave Spain and reside
in Paris. Thus the Queen of France would
be the Queen of Spain. In fact, Spain would
be annexed to France as a sort of tributary nation, the court being at Paris, and all the offices being at the disposal of the Queen of
France, residing there. The pride of the Span-

iards revolted from this, and still the diploma-
tists were conferring upon the matter.

Henrietta, the unfortunate widow of Charles
I. of England, had an elder daughter, who had
married the Prince of Orange, the head of the
illustrious house of Nassau. This Princess of
Orange was very beautiful, young, in the enjoyment of vast possessions, and a widow. She
aspired to the hand, and to share the crown of
the King of France. Surrounded by great
magnificence and blazing with jewels, she visited the court of Louis XIV. Her mission was
signally unsuccessful. The king took a strong
dislike to her, and repelled her advances with
marked discourtesy.

While matters were in this state, Charles II.
offered his hand to Mary Mancini. But the
proud cardinal would not allow his niece to
marry a crownless and impoverished king. In
the mean time, Mary Mancini, by her increasing beauty and her mental superiority, was
gaining daily more influence over the mind of
the king. With a voice of singular melody,
a brilliant eye, a figure as graceful and elastic
as that of a fairy, and with words of wonderful wisdom flowing, as it were, instinctively
from her lips, she seemed effectually and al-

most unconsciously to have enthralled the king.
All his previous passions were boyish and
ephemeral. But Mary was very different from
any other lady of the court. Her depth of
feeling, her pensive yet cheerful temperament,
and her full-souled sympathy in all that was
truly noble in conduct and character, astonished and engrossed the susceptible monarch.

The Duchess of Savoy had a daughter, Marguerite, whom she wished to have become the
wife of the French king. The princess was
by birth of the highest rank, being a descend-
ant of Henry IV. The duchess sent as an envoy a young Piedmontese count to treat secretly with the cardinal for the marriage of the
king with the Princess Marguerite. The count
was unsuccessful. It was quite evident that
Mazarin was intending to secure the marriage
of the king with his niece.

The proud queen, Anne of Austria, became
greatly alarmed. She mortally offended the
cardinal by declaring to him that nothing
should induce her to consent to such a degradation of her son as to permit his marriage
with the niece of the cardinal. She declared
that in such an event she herself would head
an insurrection against the king, and that the

whole of France would revolt both against him
and his minister.   These bitter words ever after rankled in the bosom of the cardinal.

The queen summoned a secret assembly of
the cabinet, and put to them the question
whether the marriage of her son without her
consent would be a valid one.   The unanimous
decision was in the negative.   She then had
this decision carefully drawn up, and made effectual arrangements to have it registered by
the Parliament, should the king secretly marry Mary Mancini.

The cardinal now found himself compelled
to abandon his ambitious hopes for his niece,
and opened again negotiations with Spain for
the hand of the Infanta Maria Theresa, and
with the court of Savoy for the Princess Marguerite.   The Spanish marriage would termi-
nate the war.   The union with Savoy would
invest France with new powers for its vigorous
prosecution.

Every day the attachment of the king to
Mary Mancini became more undisguised.   She
guided his reading; she taught him the Italian
language; she introduced to him the names of
great men in the works of literature and art,
and labored heroically to elevate his tastes, and

to inspire him with the ambition of performing glorious deeds.

The queen, in her anxiety, made arrangements for the king to meet the Princess Marguerite at Lyons, that they might be betrothed.
She greatly preferred the alliance with Spain;
but as there seemed to be insuperable objec-
tions to that, she turned her attention to Savoy.
The king continued his marked and almost exclusive attentions to Mary, and she loved him
with the full flow of her ardent affections.

The whole court was to proceed in great
magnificence to Lyons, to meet the court of
Savoy. Mary was compelled to accompany
the court. She knew full well the errand
upon which Louis was bound. Though her
heart was heavy, and tears dimmed her eyes,
she was obliged to appear cheerful. She had
made an earnest effort to avoid the journey,
but Anne of Austria was obdurate and cruel.
She assured Mary that she could not spare her
presence when she wished to impress the Princess Marguerite with the magnificence and
beauty of the French court.

The court of Savoy left Turin at the same
time that the French court left Paris. The
pledge had been given that, should the king be

pleased with the appearance of Marguerite, the marriage should take place without delay. During the journey, the heartless and fickle king, ever charmed by novelty, was in buoyant spirits. Though he still clung to the side of Mary, giving her a seat in his own carriage, and, when the weather was fine, riding by her side on horseback, he tortured her heart by the joyousness with which he spoke of the antici- pated charms of Marguerite and of his ap- proaching marriage.

At Lyons the royal party was received with great magnificence. The next day it was an- nounced that the court of Savoy was approach- ing. The queen-mother and her son, with two ladies in the royal coach, preceded, and, follow- ed by a considerable retinue, advanced to meet their guests. The king mounted his horse and galloped forward to get a sight of Marguerite without being known by her. She was riding in an open barouche. He soon returned in great glee, and, springing from the saddle, re- entered the carriage, and informed his mother that the Princess Marguerite was very beauti- ful. Scarcely had he said this ere the two royal coaches met. Both parties alighted. The princess was introduced to Louis. Then

the queen-mother and her son, the Duchess of
Savoy and the Princess Marguerite, and an
elder daughter, who was a widow, entered the
royal coach and returned to Lyons. The king
was in exuberant spirits. He at once entered
into the most animated and familiar conversation with the princess.

The Princess Marguerite fully appreciated
the embarrassment of her own situation. She
was going to Lyons to present herself to Louis
XIV. to see if he would take her for his wife.
The humiliation of being rejected would be
dreadful. In vain she implored her mother
to spare her from such a possibility. But the
question seemed to be at once settled favora-
bly. The king was manifestly much pleased
with Marguerite, and the princess could see
nothing but attractions in the young, handsome, and courtly sovereign of France.

Poor Mary, who was informed of every thing
that transpired, was suffering martyrdom. She
was immediately forsaken and forgotten. In
public, all her force of character was called
into requisition to dress her face in smiles. In
her secret apartment she wept bitterly.

CHAPTER IV.

THE MARRIAGE OF THE KING.

THE Princess Marguerite of Savoy was very beautiful. She was a brunette, with large, lustrous eyes, fairy-like proportions, queenly bearing, and so graceful in every movement that she scarcely seemed to touch the ground as she walked. Her reception by the king, the queen, and the whole court was every thing that could be desired. The duchess and her daughter that night placed their heads upon their pillows with the undoubting conviction that Marguerite was to be the Queen of France. The king ordered his suite to be ready, in their gala dresses, to attend him on the morrow to the apartments of the princess.

The morning came. To the surprise and bewilderment of the court, every thing was changed. The king was thoughtful, distant, reserved. With great formality of etiquette, he called upon the princess. His countenance and manner indicated an entire change of feeling. With the coldest phrases of court etiquette

122   Louis XIV.   [1658.

An heir to the Spanish throne.   Rejection of Marguerite.

he addressed her. He was civil, and civil only.
The warmth of the lover had disappeared entirely. The Duchess of Savoy was astounded.
Even the French court seemed stupefied by so
unexpected and decisive an alteration in the
aspect of affairs.

The explanation which gradually came to
light was very simple. During the night a
courier had arrived, in breathless haste, with
the announcement that the Queen of Spain
had given birth to a son. Maria Theresa was
no longer heir to the throne. The way was
consequently open to the Spanish marriage.
This alliance would secure peace with Spain,
and was altogether a more powerful and
wealthy connection than that with the court
of Savoy. The cardinal immediately communicated the intelligence to the queen-mother
and the king. They alone knew it. Marguerite was to be rejected, and the hand of Maria
Theresa to be claimed.

Mary Mancini was utterly bewildered by the
change, so inexplicable to her, in the posture of
affairs. The face of the queen was radiant with
joy. The king seemed a little embarrassed, but
very triumphant. The Duchess of Savoy betrayed alternately surprise, indignation, and de-

spair.   The eagle eye and painful experience
of Mary taught her that the Princess Marguerite was struggling to retain her self-possession,
and to maintain a cheerful spirit, while some
terrible blow had fallen upon her.

The news from Spain was such that Mazarin,
upon receiving it after midnight, hastened to
the bedchamber of the queen with the announcement.   As he entered, the queen rose
upon her pillow, and the cardinal said :

"I have come to tell you, madame, a piece of
news which your majesty never anticipated."

"Is peace proclaimed ?" inquired the queen,
earnestly.

"More than peace," the cardinal exultantly
replied ; "for the Infanta brings peace in her
hand as but a portion of her dower."

This extraordinary scene took place on the
night of the 29th of November, 1658.   It was
the task of the wily cardinal to break the humiliating intelligence to the Duchess of Savoy.
He assured her that he felt bound to seek,
above all things else, the interests of France;
that an opportunity had unexpectedly occurred
for an alliance with Spain ; that this alliance
was far more desirable than any other ; but that,
should any thing occur to interrupt these nego-

tiations, he would do every thing in his power
to promote the marriage of the king with the
Princess Marguerite.

Notwithstanding the intense irritation which
this communication excited, there was too much
self-respect and too much good breeding in the
court of Savoy to allow of a sudden rupture,
which would provoke the sarcastic remarks of
the world. Still the duchess, in a private interview with Mazarin, could not restrain her
feelings, but broke out into passionate upbraid-
ings. The thought that she had been lured to
expose herself and her daughter to the derision
of all Europe stung her to the quick. The
Princess Marguerite, however, by her graceful
composure, by her courtesy to all around her,
and by the skill with which she concealed her
wounded feelings, won the admiration of all
in both courts.

For several days the two courts remained
together, engaged in a round of festivities.
This seemed necessary to avoid the appearance of an open rupture. The fickle king, in
these assemblies, treated Marguerite with his
customary courtesy; but he immediately turned
to Mary Mancini with his marked attentions
and devotion, dancing with her repeatedly on

the same evening, and keeping her constantly
by his side. Indeed, his attentions were so
very marked as to lead the courtiers to think
that the king rejoiced at his escape from his
marriage with Marguerite from the hope that
it might yet lead to his securing Mary for his
bride. But it is more probable that the king,
utterly selfish, reckless of the feelings of others,
and devoted to his own enjoyment, sought the
society of Mary because it so happened that she
was the one, more than any other then within
his reach, who, by her personal beauty and her
mental attractions, could best beguile his weary
hours. He was ready at any moment, without
a pang, to lay her aside for another who could
better minister to his pleasure or to the aspir-
ings of his ambition.

The king, with his court, returned to Paris.
The secret communicated by the mysterious
visitor from Spain was still undivulged. The
mystery was so great, and its apparent bearing
upon the destiny of Mary so direct, that she
resolved to interrogate one of the most influential ministers of the court upon the subject.
He, thinking in some degree to evade the question, replied that the courier had come simply
to inform Anne of Austria that the Queen of

Spain had given birth to a son. This revealed the whole to Mary.

In the mean time, arrangements were made
for Cardinal Mazarin to meet the Spanish
minister on the frontiers of the two kingdoms
to negotiate for the Spanish marriage. The
cardinal, fully convinced that now it would be
impossible to secure the hand of the king for
his niece Mary, and anxious to convince the
queen that he was heartily engaged in promoting the Spanish alliance, ordered Mary immediately to withdraw from the court, and retire to Brouage. This was a fortified town on
the sea-coast many leagues from Paris. The
king heard of the arrangement, and, forbidding
the departure of Mary from the court, hastened to the cardinal demanding an explanation.
Mazarin informed him that the Infanta of
Spain would be very indignant should she
learn that, while he was making application for
her hand, he was retaining near him one whom
he had long treated with the most devoted and
affectionate attentions; that her father, Philip
IV., would be disgusted; that there would be
a probable rupture of the negotiations; and
that the desolating war between France and
Spain would continue.

Louis declared that he should not allow his pleasure to be disturbed by such considerations. Roused by opposition, he went so far as to say that he was quite ready to carry on the war with Spain if that power so wished; that the war would afford him an opportunity to acquire glory in the eyes of his countrymen, and in that case he would marry Mary Mancini.

But the cardinal was fully conscious that neither the queen nor France would now submit to such an arrangement. He had with great skill retained his attitude of command over the young monarch, holding his purse and governing the realm, while the boy-king amused himself as a ballet-dancer and a play-actor. The cardinal remained inexorable. It is said that the king wept in the excess of his chagrin as he felt compelled to yield to the representations of his domineering minister. As he unfolded to him the miseries which would be inflicted, not only upon the kingdom, but upon the court, should the desolating and expensive war be protracted, the king threw himself upon a sofa, and buried his face in his hands in silent despair. It was decided that Mary should be exiled from the court.

The king, thwarted, vexed, wretched, repair-

ed to the cabinet of his mother. They conversed for an hour together. As they retired
from the cabinet, Madame de Motteville says,
"the eyes of both were red with weeping. The
orders were immediately issued for Mary's departure. She was to go with an elder sister
and her governess. The morrow came; the
carriage was at the door. Mary, having taken
leave of the queen, repaired to the apartment
of Louis to bid him adieu. She found him
deluged in tears. Summoning all her resolution to maintain self-control, she held out her
trembling hand, and said to him reproach-
fully, 'Sire, you are a king; you weep; and
yet I go.'"

The king uttered not a word, but, burying
his face in his hands upon the table, sobbed
aloud. Mary saw that it was all over with
her; that there was no longer any hope. Without speaking a word, she descended the stairs
to her carriage. The king silently followed
her, and stood by the coach door. She took
her seat with her companions, and, without the
interchange of a word or a sign, the carriage
drove away. Louis remained upon the spot
until it disappeared from sight.

The Isle of Pheasants, a small Spanish isl-

ISLE OF PHEASANTS.

1—9

and in the Bidassoa, a boundary river between
France and Spain, was fixed upon as the rendezvous for the contracting parties for the
royal marriage. Four days after the exile of
Mary, the king and court, with a magnificent
civil and ecclesiastical retinue, set out for the
island. The king insisted, notwithstanding the
vehement remonstrances of the queen, upon
visiting Mary Mancini on the journey. As
the splendid cortége passed through the streets
of Paris, the whole population was on the pave-
ment, shouting a thousand blessings on the head
of their young king.

Mary Mancini had received orders from the
queen to proceed with her sister to Saint Jean
d'Angély, where, upon the passage of the court,
she was to have an interview with the king.
" Her interview," writes Miss Pardoe, " was,
however, a bitter one. Divided between vanity and affection, Louis was at once less firm
and less self-possessed than Mary. He wept
bitterly, and bewailed the fetters by which he
was shackled. But as he remarked the change
which nights of watching and of tears had
made in her appearance, he felt half consoled.
The only result of this meeting was to harrow
the heart of the poor victim of political expe-

diency, and to prove to her upon how unstable
a foundation she had built her superstructure
of hope."*

From Saint Jean d'Angély the court proceeded, by way of Bordeaux, to Toulouse.
Here they awaited the conclusion of the treaty.
The negotiation was tedious, as each party was
anxious to gain all that was possible from the
other. Many questions of national moment
and pride were involved. At length the conference was amicably concluded. The king
agreed to pardon the Prince of Condé, and restore to him all his honors; and the Infanta
Maria Theresa renounced for herself and her
descendants all claim to the inheritance of her
parents. She was to receive as a dowry five
hundred thousand golden crowns. There were
several other articles included in the treaty
which have now ceased to be of any interest.

Much surprise was soon excited in the court
of Louis XIV. by the intimation that the marriage ceremony must be postponed until the
spring. Philip IV. stated that his infirm health
would not allow him to take so long a journey
in the inclement weather of winter. Louis
XIV. had never yet seen his affianced bride.

* Louis XIV. and the Court of France, vol. ii., p. 23, 24.

We do not learn that he was at all annoyed by the delay. The intervening weeks were passed in journeyings and a round of amusements. Early in May, 1660, the king returned to the vicinity of the Isle of Pheasants, where he was to meet the King of Spain and Maria Theresa.

The most magnificent preparations had been made at the Isle of Pheasants for the interview between the two courts and the royal nuptials. Bridges were constructed to the island from both the French and Spanish sides of the river. These bridges were covered, and so decorated as to present the aspect of beautiful galleries. Upon the island a palace was erected, consisting of one immense and gorgeous apartment, with lateral chambers and dressing-rooms. This apartment was carpeted, and furnished with all the splendor which the combined monarchies of France and Spain could command.

Two doors, directly opposite each other, enabled the two courts to enter simultaneously. A straight line across the centre of the room divided it into two portions, one half of which was regarded as French, and the other as Spanish territory. The Spanish court took up its residence at Fontarabia, on the eastern or Spanish bank of the river. Louis and his court oc cupied Saint Jean de Luz, on the French or western side of the stream.

There are many exactions of court etiquette which to republican eyes seem extremely irrational and foolish. Louis could not cross the river to take his Spanish bride, neither could Maria Theresa cross the stream to be married on French soil; therefore Don Luis de Haro, as the proxy of Louis XIV., having the French Bishop of Frejus as his witness, was married to Maria Theresa in the church at Fontarabia. The ceremony was conducted with the most punctilious observance of the stately forms of Spanish etiquette.

Madame de Motteville gives the following account of the appearance of the bride:

"The Infanta is short, but well made. We admired the extreme fairness of her complexion. The blue eyes appeared to us to be fine, and charmed us by their softness and brilliancy. We celebrated the beauty of her mouth, and of her somewhat full and roseate lips. The outline of her face is long, but, being rounded at the chin, pleased us. Her cheeks, rather large, but handsome, had their share of our praise. Her hair, of a very light auburn, accorded admirably with her fine complexion."

The Infanta was dressed in white satin, ornamented with small bows of silver serge. She wore a large number of brilliant gems, and her head was decorated with a mass of false hair. The first lady of her household bore her train.

During the ceremony Philip IV. stood between his daughter and the proxy of Louis. The princess did not present her hand to Don Luis, nor did he present to her the nuptial ring. At the close of the ceremony the father embraced his child, and silently the gorgeous train swept from the church.

The next day Anne of Austria, accompanied by her second son, then Duke of Orleans, repaired to the Isle of Pheasants to meet her brother, Philip IV., and the royal bride. Court etiquette did not yet allow Louis XIV. to have an interview with the lady to whom he was already married by proxy. He, however, sent to his young queen, by one of his nobles, a present of some very fine jewels.

Though Philip IV. was the brother of Anne of Austria, and though they had not met for many years, Spanish etiquette would not allow any demonstrations of tenderness. The interview was chillingly stately and dignified. Anne, for a moment forgetting the icy re-

straints of the court, in sisterly love endeavored to salute her brother on the cheek. The
Spanish king held back his head, rejecting the
proffered fondness. The young bride threw
herself upon her knees, requesting permission
to kiss the hand of Anne of Austria. The
queen-mother lifted her from the floor, and tenderly embraced her.

After some time had elapsed, Cardinal Mazarin entered, of course from the French side,
and, advancing to their majesties, informed
them that there was a distinguished stranger
at the door who begged permission to enter.
Anne and Philip affected to hold a brief conference upon the subject, when they gave their
consent for his admission.

Louis XIV. entered in regal attire to see for
the first time, and to be seen for the first time
by, his bride. As he approached, Maria Theresa fixed her eyes upon him, and blushed deeply. Philip IV. smiled graciously, and said au-
dibly to Anne of Austria, "I have a very handsome son-in-law."

As we have mentioned, there was a line sep-
arating the Spanish half of the room from the
French half. Louis advanced to the centre
of the apartment, and kneeled upon a cushion

which had been provided for him there. The
King of Spain kneeled also upon a similar
cushion. Cardinal Mazarin then brought in a
Bible, with a cross upon the volume. One of
the high Spanish church officials did the same
on his side. The treaty of peace was then
read simultaneously to Philip IV. in Spanish,
to Louis XIV. in French. At its conclusion,
they each placed their hands upon the Bible,
and took a solemn oath to observe its stipula-
tions. During this scene one sovereign was
ceremonially in France, and the other in Spain.
Having taken the oath, they rose, and in stately
strides advanced to the frontier line. Here they
cordially embraced each other.

At the conclusion of sundry other ceremonies, some tedious, some imposing, the two
courts returned each to its own side of the
river. Maria Theresa accompanied her father.
The next morning the queen-mother, with a
suitable retinue, returned to the island palace,
where she met again the bride of her son, and
conducted her to her own apartments at Saint
Jean de Luz. Two days elapsed, while preparations were made again to solemnize the marriage beneath the skies of France.

A platform was constructed, richly carpeted,

from the residence of Anne of Austria to the
church. The young maiden-queen was robed
in French attire for this repetition of the nuptial ceremony. She wore a royal mantle of
violet-colored velvet, sprinkled with fleur de
lis, over a white dress. A queenly crown was
upon her brow. Her gorgeous train was borne
by three of the most distinguished ladies of
France. At the conclusion of this ceremony
Louis XIV. received his bride. The king was
then in the twenty-second year of his age.

Until within a week of the royal marriage,
the king wrote frequently to Mary Mancini.
Then the correspondence was suddenly dropped. The king never after seemed to manifest
any interest in her fate.

After a few days of festivity, the court commenced, on the 15th of June, its leisurely return toward Paris. Having reached Vincennes,
the illustrious cortége tarried for several days
in the royal chateau there, until preparations
could be completed for a magnificent entrance
into the capital. The gorgeous spectacle took
place on the 26th of August, 1660. For many
weeks the saloons of the Louvre and the Tuileries resounded with unintermitted revelry.

Very cruelly the queen-mother sent a mes-

THE LOUVRE AND THE TUILERIES

sage to Mary Mancini, expressing her regret
that she could not be present at the royal nuptials, and requiring her to come immediately
to be present at the entrée of the king and
queen into the metropolis, and to share in the
festivities of the palace. The order came to
the crushed and bleeding heart of Mary like a
death-summons. Accompanied by her two sisters, and with suitable attendants, she set forth
on her sad journey. All France was rejoicing
over the royal marriage, and as her carriage
rapidly approached Paris, every hour pierced
her heart with a new pang. With all the for-
titude she could summon, she could not retain
the roseate glow of health and happiness. Her
cheeks were pale and emaciate, and her forced
smile only proclaimed more loudly the grief
which was consuming her heart. She alighted
at the new palace of her uncle, Cardinal Mazarin, and hastily retired to her apartment.

She had scarcely entered her room ere a letter from the cardinal was presented to her, soliciting her hand for Prince Colonna, one of the
most illustrious nobles in wealth and rank in
Europe. This marriage would give her position scarcely second to that of any lady not
seated on a throne. The ambitious cardinal,

not fully understanding the delicate mechanism of a young lady's heart, had negotiated this matter, hoping thus to rescue his niece from the humiliating sympathy of the courtiers. But the noble nature of Mary recoiled from such a rescue. She had instinctively resolved that in her own person, and by her own individual force of character, however great might be her sufferings, she would maintain her womanly dignity. Consequently, to the surprise of the cardinal, she returned a cold and positive refusal to the proposition.

Soon after this she received a communication to repair to the palace of Fontainebleau, there to be presented to the young queen, with her two sisters, and many others of the notabilities of the realm. The presentation was to take place on the ensuing Sunday, immediately after high mass. Her elder sister, the Countess de Soissons, assisted by the Princess de Conti, was to preside at the ceremony.

Mary had just entered the audience-hall, and was approaching the queen to be presented, when Louis XIV. entered the apartment to invite Maria Theresa to accompany him in a walk in the park. Just at that moment Madame de Soissons was presenting Mademoiselle *Mancini*.

The king heard the name which had once been apparently so dear to him. Without the slightest emotion or the least sign of recognition, he bowed, as if in the presence of a perfect stranger, and inquired of Mary respecting her uncle the cardinal. He then exchanged a few courteous words with the other ladies in the room with the same assumed or real indifference, and invited all the ladies of the circle to attend the queen in a hunt in which she was about to engage.

It seemed as if the fates had combined to expose poor Mary to every species of mental torture. Her brain reeled, and, scarcely able to retain her footing, she withdrew a little apart to rally her disordered senses. Unable any longer to endure these sufferings, she begged to be excused from attending the hunt, alleging that the feeble health of her uncle the cardinal rendered it necessary for her to return to Paris. Her carriage was ordered for her departure, but, at a short distance from the chateau, she encountered the whole hunting-party, filling the road with its splendor. Her carriage was compelled to stop, that the king and queen and royal train might pass.

"And thus again she saw Louis, who pre-

ceded the cavalcade on horseback, surrounded
by the nobles of his court. The heart of Mary
throbbed almost to bursting. It was impossible that the king should not recognize the liv-
ery of her uncle—the carriage in which he had
so often been seated by her side; he would not,
he *could* not pass her by without one word.
She deceived herself. His majesty was laugh-
ing at some merry tale, by which he was so
much engrossed that he rode on without even
bestowing a look upon the gilded coach and
its heart-broken occupant."*

Mary returned to Paris pondering deeply
her awful destiny. She saw that she was fated
to meet continually the king and queen in their
festivities; that with a broken heart she must
feign gayety and smiles; that by lingering torture she must sink into the grave. There was
no refuge for her but to escape from Paris and
from the court. Apparently the only way to
accomplish this was to accept the proffered
hand of the Prince Colonna, who would remove her from Paris to Rome.

The next morning, pale and tearless, Mary
drove to Vincennes, where Cardinal Mazarin
then was, and informed him that she was ready

* Louis XIV. and the Court of France, vol. ii., p. 48.

PALACE OF FONTAINEBLEAU.

1—10

to marry Prince Colonna, provided the marriage could take place immediately, and that the cardinal would, without an hour's delay, write to the king to obtain his consent. The cardinal was rejoiced, and proceeded with energy. The king, without one kind word, gave his cold and indifferent consent. In accordance with the claims of etiquette, he sent her some valuable gifts, which she did not dare to decline.

"Mary walked to the altar," says Miss Pardoe, to whom we are indebted for many of these details, "as she would have walked to the scaffold, carrying with her an annual dower of one hundred thousand livres, and perjuring herself by vows which she could not fulfill. Her after career we dare not trace. Suffice it that the ardent and enthusiastic spirit which would, had she been fated to happiness, have made her memory a triumph for her sex, embittered by falsehood, wrong, and treachery, involved her in errors over which both charity and propriety oblige us to draw a veil; and if all Europe rang with the enormity of her excesses, much of their origin may safely be traced to those who, after wringing her heart, trampled it in the dust beneath their feet."

A few days after the scenes of presentation

at Fontainebleau, the royal pair made their triumphal entry into Paris. In those days of feudal oppression and ignorance, the masses looked up to kings and queens with a degree of superstitious reverence which, in our enlightened land, seems almost inconceivable. Louis XIV. was a heartless, selfish, pleasure-loving young man of twenty-one, who had never in his life done any thing to merit the especial esteem of any one. Maria Theresa was an amiable and pretty girl, who never dreamed that she had any other function than to indulge in luxuries at the expense of others. Millions were to be impoverished that she and her husband might pass through life reveling in luxury and charioted in splendor. One can not contemplate such a state of things without being agitated by the conflicting emotions of pity for such folly and indignation for such outrages. Louis and Maria Theresa were received by the populace of Paris with as much reverence and enthusiasm as if they had been angels descending from heaven, fraught with every blessing.

Scarcely had the morning dawned ere the whole city was in commotion. The streets were thronged with countless thousands in the

most brilliant gala dresses. Triumphal arches
spanned the thoroughfares through which the
royal procession was to pass. Garlands of flowers and hangings of brilliantly colored tapestry
concealed the fronts of the houses from view.
The pavements were strewn with flowers and
sweet-scented herbs, over which the wheels of
the carriages and the hoofs of the horses would
pass without noise. At the barrier a gorgeous
throne was erected. Here the young queen
was seated in royal state, to receive the homage of the several distinguished officers of the
city and of the realm. At the close of these
ceremonies, which were rendered as imposing
as civil and ecclesiastical pomp could create,
the apparently interminable procession of carriages, and horsemen, and footmen, with the
most dazzling adornments of caparisons, and
uniforms, and banners, with resounding music,
and shouts of acclaim which seemed to rend
the skies, commenced its entrance into the city.

An antique car had been constructed, of
massive and picturesque proportions, embla-
zoned with gold. Upon this car the young
queen was seated. She was, in reality, very
beautiful, but in this hour of triumph, with
flushed cheek and sparkling eye, robed in the

richest attire, brilliant with gems, and so conspicuously enthroned as to be visible to every
eye, she presented an aspect of almost celestial
loveliness.

The young king rode by her side, magnificently mounted. His garments of velvet, richly embroidered with gold and jewels, had been
prepared for the occasion at an expense of con-
siderably more than a million of dollars. The
splendors of this gala-day were never forgotten
by those who witnessed them.

For succeeding weeks and months the court
luxuriated in one continued round of gayety
and extravagance. Night after night the magnificent saloons of the Louvre and the Tuileries
resounded with music, while proud lords and
high-born dames trod the floors in the mazy
dance, and inflamed their passions with the
most costly wines. It can not be denied that
a man who is trained from infancy amidst such
scenes could acquire elegance of manner which
those engrossed in the useful and ennobling
employments of life rarely attain. Neither
can it be denied that this is as poor a school
as can possibly be imagined to prepare one
wisely to administer the affairs of a nation of
twenty millions of people. In fact, Louis XIV.

never dreamed of consulting the interests of the people. It was his sole object to aggrandize himself by promoting the splendor, the power, and the glory of the monarchy.

One does well to be angry when he reflects that, to maintain this reckless and utterly useless extravagance of the king and the court, the millions of the peasantry of France were compelled to live in mud hovels, to wear the coarsest garb, to eat the plainest food, while their wives and their daughters toiled barefooted in the fields. One would think that guilty consciences would often be appalled by the announcement, " Know thou that for all these things God will bring thee into judgment ?"

Though this revolting state of society was the slow growth of time, and though no one there could have regarded this aristocratic oppression as it is now estimated in the clearer light of the present day, still these outrages, inflicted by the strong upon the weak, by the rich upon the poor, merit the unmitigated condemnation of men, as they have ever incurred the denunciations of God.

Cardinal Mazarin, more than any other man in France, was accountable for the enormous luxury of the court, and the squalid misery of

the people. He knew better. He was pro-
fessedly a disciple of Jesus Christ, and yet a
more thorough worldling could hardly have
been in Christian or in pagan lands. He was
one of the most gigantic robbers of the poor
of which history gives any mention.

In the midst of these festivities, Mazarin decided to invite the court to a grand ballet,
which should transcend in splendor every thing
which Paris had witnessed before. To deco-
rate the saloons, a large amount of costly draperies were manufactured at Milan. In ar-
ranging these tapestries, by some accident they
took fire. The flames spread rapidly, utterly
destroying the room, with its paintings and
its magnificently frescoed roof. The fire was
eventually extinguished, but the shock was a
death-blow to the cardinal. He was then in
feeble health. His attendants conveyed him
from the blazing room to the Chateau Mazarin.

The terror of the scene so aggravated the
maladies from which the cardinal had for a
long time suffered, that he was prostrated upon
his bed, and it soon became evident that his
dying hour was near at hand. There are many
indications that the haughty cardinal was tortured by the pangs of remorse. He was gen-

erally silent, though extremely dejected. His body was subjected to the most extraordinary convulsions, while inaudible murmurs escaped his lips.

Count de Brienne, in his memoirs, states that, on one occasion, he entered the chamber of the cardinal on tiptoe, his valet informing him that his eminence was asleep. He found Mazarin bolstered in an arm-chair before the fire, apparently in a profound slumber, "and yet," writes the count, "his body rocked to and fro with the greatest rapidity, from the back of his chair to his knees, now swinging to the right, and again to the left. These movements of the sufferer were as regular and rapid as the vibrations of the pendulum of a clock. At the same time inarticulate murmurs escaped his lips."

The count, much moved by the wretched spectacle, summoned the attendant, and awoke the cardinal. Mazarin, in awaking, betrayed that troubled state of soul which had thus agitated his body. In most melancholy tones, he said,

"My physician, M. Guénaud, has informed me that I can live but a few days."

Count de Brienne, wishing to console him,

said, "But M. Guénaud is not omniscient. He
may be deceived."

The cardinal, uttering a heavy sigh, exclaimed, "Ah! M. Guénaud well understands his
trade."

Mazarin, as we have mentioned, had acquired enormous wealth. The resources of the
kingdom had been in his hands. The poor had
been oppressed by as terrible a system of taxation as human nature could endure and live.
With the sums thus extorted, he had not only
maintained the army, and supported the vo-
luptuousness of the court, but he had also ap-
propriated vast sums, without the slightest right
to do so, to his own private enrichment. He
was now dying. The thought of going to the
bar of God with his hands full of this stolen
gold tortured him. Constrained by the anguish of a death-bed, he sent for a Theatine
monk to act as his confessor, and to administer,
in his last hours, the services of the Church.

The virtuous monk was quite startled when
the cardinal, with pale and trembling lips, informed him that he had accumulated a fortune
of over forty millions of francs—$8,000,000.
Mazarin allowed that he considered it a sin
that he had by such means accumulated such

vast wealth. His pious confessor boldly declared that the cardinal would peril his eternal
salvation if he did not, before his death, make
restitution of all his ill-gotten gains, reserving
only that for which he was indebted to the
bounty of the king.

The dying sinner, trembling in view of the
judgment, replied in faltering accents, "In
that case I must relinquish all. I have received nothing from the king. My family
must be left in utter beggary."

The confessor was deeply moved by the aspect of despair presented by the cardinal. Embarrassed by the difficulties of the position, he
sent for a distinguished member of the court,
M. Colbert, to confer with upon the situation.

The shrewd courtier, after a little delibera-
tion, suggested that, as it would be manifestly
impossible to restore the money to the different individuals, scattered all over the realm,
from whom it had been gathered in the ordinary collection of the taxes, the cardinal should
make a transfer of it, as a donation, to the sovereign. "The king," added M. Colbert, "will,
without any question, annul so generous an act,
and restore the property to you. It will then
be yours by royal grant."

The cardinal, who had lived, and moved, and
had his being in the midst of trickery and intrigue, highly approved of the suggestion. The
papers were immediately made out, transferring the property to the king. It was the 3d
of March, 1661. Three days passed, and there
was no response of rejection—no recognition
of the gift. The cardinal was terror-stricken.
As he sat bolstered in his chair, he wrung his
hands in agony, often exclaiming, "My poor
family! my poor family! they will be left
without bread."

At the close of the third day M. Colbert entered the dying chamber with a document in
his hand, announcing that the king had restored to the cardinal all his property, authoriz-
ing him.to dispose of it as he judged to be best.

It is scarcely possible that this trickery could
have satisfied the conscience of the cardinal.
His confessor professed to be satisfied, and
granted the dying man that absolution which
he had previously withheld. Still Mazarin
was extremely reluctant to die. He dressed
with the utmost care; painted his wrinkled
brow and emaciate cheeks, and resorted to all
the appliances of art to maintain the aspect of
youth and vigor. But death could not thus be

deceived. The destroying angel on the 9th of March bore his spirit away to the judgment seat of Christ. He died in the Chateau Mazarin, at the age of fifty-two, having been virtually monarch of France for eighteen years.

CHATEAU MAZARIN.

It appeared by the will of Mazarin that his property was vastly greater even than the enormous sum which he had reluctantly admitted. That portion of it which might be included under the term real estate, consisting of houses, lands, etc., amounted to over fifty millions of francs, while his personal effects, embracing the most costly furniture, diamonds, and other jewels, of which he strictly forbade any inventory to be taken, amounted to many millions more. The legacies to his nieces and to other aristocratic friends were truly princely. To the *poor* he left a miserable pittance amounting to about twelve hundred dollars.

The cardinal was a heartless, avaricious man, of but little ability, and yet endowed with a very considerable degree of that cunning which sometimes proves to be temporarily so successful in diplomatic intrigues. The king was probably glad to be rid of him, for he could not easily throw off a yoke to which he had been habituated from childhood. During most of the cardinal's illness Louis continued his usual round of feasting and dancing. Upon his death he manifested no grief. It seems that he had previously made up his mind no longer to be troubled by a prime minister, but to rule absolutely by his own will.

Two days before the death of Mazarin, when he was no longer capable of transacting any business, the president of the ecclesiastical assembly inquired of the king "to whom he must hereafter address himself on questions of public business." The emphatic and laconic response was, "*To myself.*"

CHAPTER V.

FESTIVITIES OF THE COURT.

CARDINAL MAZARIN was exceedingly unpopular both with the court and the masses of the people. Haughty, domineering, avaricious, there was nothing in his character to win the kindly regards of any one. His death gave occasion to almost universal rejoicing. Indeed, it was with some difficulty that the king repressed the unseemly exhibition of this joy on the part of the court. The cardinal, as we have mentioned, had been for many years virtually monarch of France. He, in the name of the king, imposed the taxes, appointed the ministry, issued all orders, and received all reports. The accountability was so entire to him that the monarch, immersed in pleasure, had but little to do with reference to the affairs of the realm.

Immediately upon the death of Mazarin, the king summoned to his presence Tellier, minister of War, Lionne, minister of State, and Fouquet, minister of the Treasury. He in-

Character of M. Fouquet.

formed them that he should continue them in office, but that henceforth he should dispense with the services of a prime minister, and that they would be responsible to him alone. The young king was then twenty-two years of age. He was very poorly educated, had hitherto developed no force of character, and appeared to all to be simply a frivolous, pompous, self-conceited young man of pleasure.

Fouquet had held the keys of the treasury. When the king needed money he applied to him for a supply. The almost invariable reply he received was,

"Sire, the treasury is empty, but his eminence will undoubtedly advance to your majesty a loan."

The money came, the king little cared where from while reveling in luxury, and dancing and flirting with the beauties who crowded his court.

Fouquet was an able but thoroughly unprincipled man. He had grown enormously rich by robbing the treasury. The king disliked him. But Fouquet knew that the king could not dispense with his services. He was a marvelously efficient financier, and well knew how to wrench gold from the hands of the starving millions. The property he had acquired by fraud was so great that he often outvied the king in the splendor of his establishments. Conscious of his power, he doubted not that he should still be able to hold the king, in a measure, subject to his control.

Scarcely had Louis returned from his brief conference with his ministers to his cabinet at the Louvre, ere the secretary of the deceased cardinal, M. Colbert, entered, and requested a private audience. He informed the king, to his astonishment and inexpressible delight, that the cardinal had concealed fifteen millions of money (three millions of dollars) in addition to the sums mentioned in his will; that it was doubtless his intention that this money should immediately replenish the utterly exhausted treasury of his majesty.

The king was overjoyed. He could scarcely believe the intelligence. Concealing the tidings from Fouquet, he speedily and secretly recovered the money from the several places in which it had been deposited. Fifteen millions of francs would be a large sum at any time, but two hundred years ago it was worth three or four times as much as now. Fouquet was utterly bewildered in attempting to imag-

1—11

ine where the king had obtained the sums he was so lavishly expending.

Louis XIV. by nature and by education was excessively fond of the pomp and the punctilios of court etiquette. As this new era of independence dawned upon him, it was his first and most anxious object to regulate even to the minutest details the ceremonies of the court. He was of middling stature. High-heeled shoes added between two and three inches to his height. His hair was very fine and abundant, and he wore it long, in masses of ringlets upon his shoulders. Deep blue eyes, a fair complexion, and well moulded features formed an unusually handsome countenance. He was stately in his movements, pompous in his utterance, and every word of every sentence was pronounced slowly and with distinct enunciation, as if an oracle were giving out its responses.

There was no resemblance morally, intellectually, or physically between the king and his only brother Philip. They did not love each other. During their whole lives there had been one perpetual struggle on the part of the king to domineer over his brother, and on the part of Philip to resist that domination.

Philip was gentle in disposition, effeminate in manners, and, though a voluptuary in his tastes, a man of chivalric courage. As Duke of Orleans he had large wealth, many retainers, and feudal privileges, which invested him with power which even the king was compelled to respect.

Charles II. was now King of England. The whole nation had apparently received him with exultation. Suddenly, from being a penniless and crownless wanderer, he had become a sovereign, second in rank and power to no other sovereign in Europe. His mother Henrietta, his widowed sister the Princess of Orange, and his younger sister Henrietta, of course, shared in the prosperity and elevation of Charles. They were no longer pensioners upon the charity of their French relatives, but composed the royal family of the British court.

It will be remembered how cruelly Louis treated his young cousin in the ball-room in the days of her adversity. Charles in those days had solicited of Mazarin the hand of his niece, Mary Mancini. But the proud cardinal promptly rejected the offer of a wandering prince, without purse or crown. Very soon after Charles II. ascended the throne of England, Mazarin hastened to inform him that he was ready to confer upon him his niece. Charles, a profligate fellow, declined the proffered alliance, to the great chagrin of the haughty cardinal.

Prosperity is sometimes a great beautifier. The young Princess Henrietta, upon whom the sun of prosperity was now shining in all its effulgence, seemed like a new being, radiantly lovely and self reliant. Philip fell desperately in love with her. With a form of exquisite symmetry, with the fairest complexion and lovely features, she suddenly found herself the sister of a monarch, transformed into the principal ornament, almost the central attraction, of the court. She went to England to attend the coronation of her brother. She then returned to Paris. On the 31st of March, 1661, she was married to Philip in the Palais Royal, in' the presence of the royal family and the prominent members of the court.

A few weeks after this the whole court removed to Fontainebleau. Here a month was spent in an incessant round of festivities. The fickle king, as soon as his brother had married Henrietta, saw in her new personal beauty and mental charms. It is not improbable that she

almost unconsciously, in order to avenge the
past neglect of the king, had studied all courtly graces, all endearments of manner, all conversational charms, that she might compel the
king to do justice to the fascinations of person
and character with which she was conscious
of being richly endowed. Unhappily, she was
triumphantly successful; perhaps far more so
than she had intended. The changeful and
susceptible king became completely entranced.
He was continually by her side, exasperating
Philip by his gallantry, and keenly wounding
the feelings of his young queen.

The marriage of the king with Maria Theresa had been merely a matter of state policy.
The connection had not been inspired by any
ardent affection on either side. Though the
king treated her with great politeness as the
Queen of France, her enthusiastic nature claimed a warmer sentiment from her young husband. When she saw the attentions to which
she was entitled lavished upon Henrietta, the
wife of his brother, her affectionate heart was
chilled. She became reserved, wept, sought retirement, withdrawing from all those gayeties
in which her husband attracted the attention
of the whole court by his undisguised admira-

tion for Henrietta. At last her secret anguish
so far overcame her that she threw herself,
trembling and in tears, at the feet of Anne of
Austria, and confided to her the grief of her
heart.

The queen-mother could not have been surprised at this avowal. Her eyes were open to
that which all the court beheld; and, besides,
Philip had already complained to his mother
that Louis was endeavoring to rob him of the
love of his bride. The remonstrances of the
queen-mother were of no avail. The selfish
king, ever seeking only his own pleasure, cared
little for the wreck of the happiness of others.
He devoted himself with increasing assiduity
to the society of Henrietta, frequently held his
court in her apartments, and instituted a series
of magnificent fêtes in her honor.

Philip, then Duke of Orleans, and in the enjoyment of magnificent revenues and of much
independent feudal power as brother of the
king, was designated in the court as *Monsieur*
There was at that time in the court a young
lady, one of Henrietta's maids of honor, Mademoiselle de la Vallière. Her romantic career, which subsequently rendered her famous
throughout Europe, merits a brief digression.

Louise Françoise, daughter of the Marquis de la Vallière, was born at Tours in the year 1644. She was, consequently, seventeen years of age at the time of which we write. Her father died in her infancy. Her mother, left with an illustrious name and a small income, took for a second husband a member of the court, Gaston, duke of Orleans, to whom we have previously alluded, who was brother of Louis XIII. and uncle of the king. He resided at Blois.

As the king and court were on their way to the frontiers of Spain for the marriage of Louis with Maria Theresa, it will be remembered that he stopped for a short visit to his uncle at his magnificent palace of Blois. This grand castle, with its gorgeous architectural magnificence, its shaded parks and blooming gardens, was to Louise and her many companions an earthly paradise. Here, in an incessant round of pleasures, she had passed her girlhood.

The sight of the young monarch, so graceful in figure, so handsome in features, so marvelously courteous in bearing, aroused all the enthusiasm of the susceptible young maiden of sixteen. He was her sovereign, as well as to her eyes the most fascinating specimen of a

man. She felt as though she were gazing
upon a superior, almost a celestial being. She
dreamed not of having fallen in love with him.
The feeling of admiration, and almost of ado-
ration, was altogether too elevated for earthly
passion. In the presence of the king she was
but an obscure child. In the crowded assemblage of wealth, and rank, and beauty which
greeted the king at Blois, Louise was unnoticed.
The king went on his way, leaving an impression on the heart of the young girl which could
never be effaced. She thought it would be
heaven to live in his presence, to watch his
movements, to listen to his words, even though
no word were addressed to her.

Soon after this the Duke of Orleans died.
His court was broken up. Louise was appointed to a place as one of the maids of honor of
the Princess Henrietta. She joined the court
of *Madame* in Paris just before their departure for Fontainebleau, to which place, of course,
she accompanied them.

Here, in the midst of scenes of most brilliant
festivities, Louise feasted her eyes with the sight
of the king. Louis was exceedingly fond of exhibiting his grace as a dancer. Among these
entertainments, the king took part in a ballet

with Henrietta, he, in very picturesque dress, representing the goddess Ceres. At the close of the ballet, Louise, bewildered by the scene, and oppressed by inexplicable emotions, proposed to three of her lady companions that they should take a short walk into the dim recesses of the forest. It was a brilliant night, and the cool breeze fanned their fevered cheeks. As the four young ladies retired, one of the companions of the king laughingly suggested to him that they should follow them, and learn the secret of their hearts.

The ladies seated themselves at the foot of a large tree, where they began to discuss the scenes and actors of the evening. The king and his companion, concealed at a short distance, heard every word they uttered. Louise was for a time silent, but, being appealed to upon some subject, with very emphatic utterance remarked that she wondered that they could see any body, or think of any body but the king, when he was present. Upon her companions rallying her for being so much carried away by the splendors of royalty, she declared "that it was not the king, as a *king*, who excited her admiration, but it was Louis, as the most perfect of men; that his crown added nothing to his splendor of person or mind."

The king could not see the speaker; he could only hear her enthusiastic and impassioned voice. The parties returned to the chateau. Louise was very much chagrined that she should have allowed herself so imprudently to express her feelings. She knew that the conversation would be repeated, and feared that she should become a subject of ridicule for the whole court. In the interesting account which she gives of these events in her autobiography, she says that she retired to her room and wept bitterly.

The next morning Louise repaired to the apartments of Henrietta. She was surrounded by her suite of ladies. The king was already there. As, with his accustomed gallantry, he passed down the room addressing a few words to each, he approached Louise. Her heart throbbed violently. He had never spoken to her before.

In response to his question, "And what did you think of the ballet last night?" she, greatly agitated, attempted an answer. The king observed her confusion, and instantly recognized her voice. It was the same which he

had heard the evening before in the forest expressing such enthusiastic admiration for his
person. The king started, and fixed his eyes
so intently upon her as to increase her embarrassment and attract the observation of all
around. With a profound bow the king passed
on, but again and again was seen to turn his
eyes to the blushing girl. From that time
Mademoiselle de la Vallière became the object of the marked and flattering attention of
the king.

The unaffected timidity and modesty of her
demeanor, her brilliant complexion, large and
languishing blue eyes, and profusion of flaxen
hair, were enough of themselves to excite the
admiration of one so enamored of beauty as
was Louis XIV. But, in addition to this, the
self-love of Louis was gratified by the assurance
that Louise admired him for his personal qualities, and not merely for his kingly crown.
As the king was well aware of the gossip with
which the court was filled in view of his devotion to Madame Henrietta, he perhaps deemed it expedient, by special attention to Louise,
to divert the current of thought and conversation.

A few days after this a great hunt took place

in the park. It was a hot summer's day. At
the close of the hunt a table was spread loaded with delicacies. As the king and the courtiers, in the keenest enjoyment of the merry
scene, were partaking of the sumptuous repast,
almost unobserved a thunder-cloud arose, and
there descended upon them a flood of rain so
deluging that the company scattered in all directions for shelter. Louise running, she knew
not where, soon found the king by her side.
Politely taking her by the hand, he hurried
her to a large tree, whose dense canopy of
leaves promised some protection from the
shower. There they stood, the young and
handsome king, the beautiful maiden, the rain
falling upon them in floods. It is interesting
to record that the homage which rank paid to
beauty was such that the king stood bare-
headed, with his plumed hat in his hand, engaged during the hour the rain descended in
animated conversation. After this it was observed that in the evening drives in the park
he would ride on horseback for a short time
by the carriage of the queen, or of the Princess Henrietta, and would then gallop to the
coach of Louise.

He soon commenced a daily correspondence

with her. Louis was by no means a well-ed-
ucated man. In fact, he might be almost regarded as illiterate; but his letters were written with so much delicacy of sentiment and
elegance of expression, that Louise was embarrassed in knowing how to return suitable re-
plies. She was mortified at the thought of
having her awkward letters compared with the
elegant epistles which she received. In her
embarrassment, she applied to the Marquis of
Dangeau, a man of superior talents and culture, to write her responses for her.

Louise was a very noble girl, frank, sincere,
confiding. On one occasion, when the king
was complimenting her upon the rare beauty
of her letters, the artless child confessed that
she was not the author of them, but that they
were written by the Marquis of Dangeau.
The king smiled, and had the grace to admit
that his letters to her were written by the same
individual!

It had become a common entertainment of
the court to put up in a lottery some beautiful
article of jewelry. On one occasion the king
drew a very costly pair of bracelets. All were
looking with some curiosity to see to whom he
would present them. Pausing for a moment,

the king admiringly contemplated the sparkling gems, and then, threading his way through
the throng of ladies, advanced to Mademoiselle
de la Vallière, who stood a little apart, and
placed them in her hands. Henrietta turned
pale, and bit her lip with vexation. The queen,
Maria Theresa, looked on with a marble smile,
which revealed nothing of her feelings. Louise
was embarrassed, but with admirable tact she
assumed that the king had merely presented
them to her for inspection. After carefully
examining them, she handed them back to him,
saying, with a courtesy, " They are indeed very
beautiful." Louis, instead of receiving them,
said, with a stately bow, " In that case, mademoiselle, they are in hands too fair to resign
them," and returned to his seat.

As we have mentioned, the minister of the
treasury was rolling in ill-gotten wealth. His
palace of Vaux,* upon which he had expended
fifteen millions of francs, eclipsed in splendor

* The chateau of Vaux was a spacious and magnificent
palace in the small village of Maincy, about three miles from
Melun. M. Fouquet purchased it, and expended enormous
sums in enlarging the buildings, ornamenting the gardens,
and decorating the walls with paintings. His expenditures
were so lavish that the chateau exceeded in magnificence
any of the royal palaces.

the royal palaces of Fontainebleau and Saint Germain. The king disliked him as a man. He knew very well that he was robbing the treasury, and it was annoying to have a subject live in state surpassing that of the sovereign. M. Fouquet very imprudently invited Louis and all his court to a magnificent fête at his chateau. All the notabilities of France were bidden to this princely festival, which the minister resolved should surpass, in splendor, any thing that France had hitherto witnessed.

The king, with an imposing escort, reached the gates of the chateau. Fouquet met him there, and conducted him and all the court, first, to the park. Here a spectacle of splendor presented itself which astonished the king. Notwithstanding all he had heard of the gorgeousness of his minister's palace, he was still not prepared for such a scene of luxury and enchantment. Instead of being gratified, he turned to Fouquet, and said to him bitterly,

" I shall never again, sir, venture to invite you to visit me. You would find yourself inconvenienced."

Fouquet felt the keen rebuke. For a moment he turned pale. He soon, however, rallied, and did all in his power to gratify his

guests by the gorgeous spectacles and sumptuous entertainments of his more than regal
home.   The king, led by his host, passed
through all the apartments of the chateau, and
acknowledged that in its interior adornings
there was not probably another edifice in Eu
rope which could equal it in magnificence.

CHATEAU DE VAUX.

In the evening there was a ball in the grand
saloon of the castle.   The king having danced
several times with Louise, she became fatigued,
and expressed the desire to leave, for a short
time, the heated room.   Louis drew her arm

through his own, and, conducting her through
the magnificent suite of apartments, which had
already excited his displeasure, pointed out to
her the armorial bearings of the proud minister, which were conspicuous in every room.
The shield represented a squirrel ascending
the topmost branches of a tree, with the motto
" *quo non ascendam.*"

Neither the king nor his fair companion understood Latin. Just then the king's secretary,
M. Colbert, entered. He hated Fouquet. He
had already detected the minister in many fal-
sifications of the treasury accounts, and had
explained the robbery to the king. Louis had
been for some time contemplating the arrest
of Fouquet, but hardly dared, as yet, to strike
one so powerful.

As M. Colbert entered, Louise inquired of
him the significance of the motto.

"It signifies," he replied, " *to what height
may I not attain,* and this significance is well
understood by those who know the boldness of
the squirrel or that of his master."

Just at that moment another courtier came
up, who remarked, " Your majesty has probably not observed that in every instance the
squirrel is pursued by a serpent."

1—12

The king turned pale with anger, and ordered the captain of his musketeers to attend him.
Louise understood full well what this meant.
She threw herself at his feet, and entreated
him not to sully his reputation by arresting a
man whose guest he was, and who was entertaining him and his court with the highest honors. With the greatest difficulty, the king was
dissuaded from immediate action. For a time
he smothered his vengeance, and the court returned to Fontainebleau.

The king's displeasure not only remained
unabated, but increased with added evidence
of the pride, display, and fraudulent transac-
tions of his minister. At length he ordered
him to be secretly arrested, conveyed in close
confinement to Angers, while a seal was placed
on all his property. But for the interposition
of the kind-hearted Louise, the degraded minister would have lost his life. It was easy for
the king, immersed in pleasure, to forget the
miserable. M. Fouquet was left in his imprisonment, almost as entirely lost to the world
as if he had been consigned to the *oubliettes*
of the Bastile.

Soon after this, the 1st of November, 1661,
Maria Theresa gave birth to a dauphin. Louis

was greatly elated. Still, the pride which he took in the child as the heir to the throne did not secure for his neglected wife any more tenderness of regard. He treated her with great courtesy, while his affections were vibrating between Henrietta and Louise. Every thing seemed to combine to magnify the power of the king. Still, the pleasure-loving monarch, while apparently wholly resigning himself to the career of a voluptuary, was with instinctive sagacity striving to undermine the resources of the haughty nobility, and to render his own court the most magnificent in Europe.

For several months the court continued immersed in gayety. Dancing, in all variety of costumes, was the great amusement of the king. There were balls every evening. Mademoiselle de la Vallière became more and more the object of the marked attentions of Louis. All his energies seemed absorbed in the small-talk of gallantry; still there were occasional indications that there were latent forces in the mind of the king which events might yet develop.

One evening the king was attending a brilliant ball in the apartments of Henrietta. As he was earnestly engaged in conversation with the beautiful Louise, some important dispatches

were placed in his hands. He seated himself
at a table to examine them. Many eyes watched his countenance as he silently perused the
documents. It was observed at one moment
that he turned deadly pale, and bit his lip with
vexation. Having read the dispatches to the
end, he angrily crushed them in his hand, and
said to several of the officers of the court who
were around him,

" Our embassador in London has been publicly insulted by the Spanish embassador."
Then turning to M. Tellier, the Minister of
War, he said, " Let my embassador at Madrid
leave that city immediately. Order the Spanish envoy to quit Paris within twenty-four
hours. The conferences at Flanders are at an
end. Unless Spain publicly recognizes the
superiority of our crown, she may prepare for
a renewal of the war."

These orders of the king created general
consternation. It was virtually inaugurating
another war, with all its untold horrors. M.
Tellier seemed thunderstruck. The king, per-
ceiving his hesitation, said to him imperiously,

" Do you not understand my orders? I
wish you immediately to assemble the council.
I will meet them in an hour."

Relationship of the French and Spanish courts.

The king then returned to the ladies, and entered into trifling small-talk with them, as if nothing of moment had occurred.

It seems that a dispute had arisen in London between the French and Spanish embassadors upon the point of precedence. This had led to a bloody rencounter in the streets between the retinues of the two ministers. The French were worsted. The Spaniards gained the contested point.

The King of Spain was the brother of Anne of Austria. His first wife, the mother of Maria Theresa, was sister of Louis XIII., and consequently aunt of Louis XIV. Thus there was a peculiar bond of relationship between the French and Spanish courts. Still Louis was unrelenting in the vigorous action upon which he had entered. In addition to the hostile measures already adopted, a special messenger was sent to Philip IV. to inform him that, unless he immediately recognized the supremacy of the French court, and made a formal apology for the insult offered the French minister, war would ensue. The Spanish king, unwilling, for so trivial a cause, to involve the two nations in a bloody conflict, very magnanimously yielded to the requirements demanded by the hot blood and wounded pride of his son-in-law. In the presence of all the foreign ministers and the assembled court at Fontainebleau, the Spanish embassador made a humble apology, and declared that never again should the precedence of the embassador of France be denied.

A very similar difficulty occurred a short time after at Rome. The French embassador there, the Duke of Créqui, an old feudal noble, accompanied by troops of retainers armed to the teeth, had, by his haughty bearing, become extremely unpopular both with the court and the people of Rome. The myrmidons of the duke were continually engaged in night-brawls with the police. On one occasion they even attacked, sword in hand, the Pope's guard, and put them to flight. The brother of Pope Alexander VII., who hated Créqui, instigated the guard to take revenge. In an infuriated mob, they surrounded the palace of the embassador, and fired upon his carriage as it entered his court-yard. A page was killed, and several other attendants wounded. Créqui immediately left the city, accusing the Pope of instigating the outrage.

Louis XIV. demanded reparation, and the

most humble apology. The proud Pope was not disposed to yield to his insolent demands. Affairs assumed so threatening an aspect, that the Pope ordered two of the guard, one an officer, to be hung, and the Mayor of Rome, who was accused of having instigated the outrage, to be banished. This concession, however, by no means satisfied the irascible Louis. He commenced landing troops in Italy, threatening to besiege Rome. The Pope appealed to the Roman Catholic princes of Germany for aid. They could not come to his rescue, for they were threatened with war by the Turks. The unhappy Pope was thus brought upon his knees. He was compelled to banish from Rome his own brother, Don Mario Chigi, and to send an embassador to Paris with the most humble apology.

These events were but slight episodes in the gay life of the pleasure-loving king. He was still reveling in an incessant round of feasting and dancing, flitting with his gay court from one to another of his metropolitan and rural palaces.

There are few so stern as not to feel emotions of sympathy rather than of condemnation for Louise de la Vallière. She was a

184   Louis XIV.   [1662.

Remorse of De la Vallière.   Illness of Anne of Austria.

child of seventeen, exposed to all the fascinations and temptations of the most luxurious
court then upon the globe. But God has im-
planted in every bosom a sense of right and
wrong. She wept bitterly over her fall. Her
remorse was so great that she withdrew as far
as possible from society, and the anguish of
her repentance greatly embarrassed her royal
lover.

Henrietta was greatly annoyed at the pref-
erence which the king had shown for Louise
over herself. She determined to drive the unfortunate favorite from the court. Anne of
Austria, with increasing years, was growing
oblivious of her own youthful indiscretions,
and was daily becoming more stern in her
judgments. A cancer had commenced its secret ravages upon her person. Its progress no
medical skill could arrest. She tried to conceal the terrible secret which was threatening
her with the most loathsome and distressing
of deaths. In this mood of mind the haughty
queen sent for the weeping Louise to her room.
Trembling in every nerve, the affrighted child
attended the summons. She found Anne of
Austria with Henrietta by her side. The
queen, without assigning any cause, sternly in-

formed her that she was banished from the
court of France, and that suitable attendants
would immediately convey her to a distant
castle. Upon Louise attempting to make
some inquiry why she was thus punished, the
haughty queen sternly interrupted her with
the reply "that France could not have two
queens."

Louise staggered back to her room overwhelmed with despair. Both God and man
will declare that, whatever fault there might
have been in the relations then existing between the king and this unprotected girl, the
censure should have rested a thousand fold
more heavily upon the king than upon his victim. And yet Louise was to be driven in ig-
nominy from the court, to enter into a deso-
lated world utterly ruined. Through the remainder of the day no one entered her apartment. She spent the hours in tears and in the
fever of despair. In the evening Louis himself came to her room and found her exhausted with weeping. He endeavored to ascertain
the cause of her overwhelming distress. She,
unwilling to be the occasion of an irreconcila-
ble feud between the mother and the son,
evaded all his inquiries. He resorted to en-

treaties, reproaches, threats, but in vain. Irritated by her pertinacious refusal, he suddenly left her without speaking a word of adieu.

Louise seemed now truly to be alone in the world, without a single friend left her. But she then recalled to mind that she had formerly entered into an agreement with the king that, in case of any misunderstanding arising between them, a night should not pass without an attempt at reconciliation. A new hope arose in her mind that the king would either return, or send her a note to inform her that his anger no longer continued.

" And so she waited and watched, and counted every hour as it was proclaimed from the belfry of the palace. But she waited and watched in vain. When at length, after this long and weary night, the daylight streamed through the silken curtains of her chamber, she threw herself upon her knees, and praying that God would not cast away the victim who was thus rejected by the world, she hastened, with a burning cheek and a tearless eye, to collect a few necessary articles of clothing, and throwing on her veil and mantle, rushed down a private staircase and escaped into the street. In this distracted state of mind she pursued

her way to Chaillot,* and reached the convent
of the Sisters of St. Mary, where she was de-
tained some time in the parlor. At length
the grating was opened and a portress appeared. On her request to be admitted to the abbess, she informed her that the community
were all at their devotions, and could not see
any one.

"It was in vain that the poor fugitive entreated and asserted her intention of taking
the vows. She could extort no other answer,
and the portress withdrew, leaving her sitting
on a wooden bench desolate, heart-sick. For
two hours she remained motionless, with her
eyes fixed upon the grating, but it continued
closed. Even the dreary refuge of this poor
and obscure convent was denied her. Even
the house of religion had barred its doors
against her. She could bear up no longer.
From the previous evening she had not tasted
food, and the fatigue of body and anguish of

* Chaillot was a village on the banks of the Seine, about
a mile and a half from the Tuileries, near the present bridge
of Jena. The nuns of the order of St. Mary had a celebrated convent here, where persecuted grandeur often sought an
asylum. Within the walls of this convent the widowed
queen of Charles I. and daughter of Henry IV. died in the
year 1669.

mind which she had undergone, combined with this unaccustomed fast, had exhausted her slight remains of strength. A sullen torpor gradually overcame her faculties, and eventually she fell upon the paved floor cold and insensible."*

The king had probably passed a very uncomfortable night. Early in the morning he learned that Louise had disappeared. Much alarmed, he hastened to the apartments of Madame Henrietta in the Tuileries. She unfeelingly expressed entire ignorance of the movements of Mademoiselle de la Vallière. He immediately repaired to the rooms of his mother. She was unable to give him any information respecting the lost favorite. Bitterly, however, she reproached her son with his want of self-control in allowing himself to cherish so strong an attachment to Mademoiselle de la Vallière. She accused him of having no mastery over himself.

The king's eyes flashed with indignation. He was fully convinced that his mother was in some way the cause of the departure of Louise. Angrily he replied,

"It may be so that I do not know how to

* Louis XIV. and the Court of France, vol. ii., p. 125.

control myself, but I will at least prove that I know how to control those who offend me."

Turning upon his heel, he left the apartment. By some means he obtained a clew to the retreat of Louise. Mounting his horse, accompanied by a single page, he galloped to the convent of Chaillot. As there had been no warning of his approach, the grating still remained closed. He arrived just after the poor girl had fallen from the wooden bench upon the tesselated floor of the cold and cheerless anteroom. Her beautiful form lay apparently lifeless before him. Tears fell profusely from his eyes. He chafed her hands and temples. In endearing terms he entreated her to awake. Gradually she revived. Frankly she related the cause of her departure, and entreated him to permit her to spend the remainder of her saddened life buried in the cloisters of the convent.

The king insisted, with all his authority as a monarch, and with all his persuasive influence as a man, that Louise should return with him to the Louvre. He was inspired with the double passion of love for her, and anger against those who had driven her from his court. Louise, saddened in heart and crushed in spirit, with great reluctance at last yielded to his

pleadings. The page was dispatched for a carriage. Seated by the side of the king, Mademoiselle de la Vallière returned to the palace,
from which she supposed a few hours before
she had departed forever. Louis immediately
repaired to the apartment of Madame Henrietta, and so imperiously insisted that Louise
should be restored to her place as one of her
maids of honor, that his sister-in-law dared not
refuse. The influence of Anne of Austria was
now nearly at an end. She was dying of slow
disease, and, notwithstanding all her efforts to
conceal the loathsome malady which was de-
vouring her, she was compelled to spend most of
her time in the seclusion of her own chamber.

Louis XIV., in the exercise of absolute power, with all the court bowing before him in the
most abject homage, had gradually begun to
regard himself almost as a God. He had nev-
·er recovered from the mortification which he
had experienced at the palace of Vaux, in finding a subject living in splendor which outvied
that of the crown. He determined to rear a
palace of such extraordinary magnificence that
no subject, whatever might be his resources,
could equal it. For some time he had been
looking around for the site of the building,

which he had resolved should, like the Pyramids, be a monument of his reign, and excite the wonder and admiration of future ages.

About twelve miles from Paris there was a little village of Versailles, surrounded by an immense forest, whose solemn depths frequently resounded with the baying of the hounds of hunting-parties, as the gayly dressed court swept through the glades.

On one occasion, Louis XIV., in the eagerness of the chase, became separated from most of the rest of the party. Night coming on, he was compelled, and the few companions with him, to take refuge in a windmill, where they remained till morning. The mill was erected upon the highest point of ground. The king caused a small pavilion to be erected there for his accommodation, should he again chance to be overtaken by night or a storm. Pleased with the position, the king ere long removed the pavilion, and ordered his architect, Lemercier, to erect upon the spot an elegant chateau according to his own taste. A landscape gardener was also employed to ornament the grounds. The region soon was embellished with such loveliness as to charm every beholder. It became the favorite rural resort of the king.

The chateau and its grounds soon witnessed a series of festivities, the fame of which resounded through all Europe. Republican America will ponder the fact, which the aristocratic courts of Europe ignored, that these entertainments of boundless extravagance were at the expense of the overtaxed and starving people. That king and courtiers might riot in luxury, the wives and daughters of peasants were harnessed by the side of donkeys to drag the plow.

Early in the spring of 1664, the king, accompanied by his court of six hundred individuals, gentlemen and ladies, with a throng of servants, repaired to Versailles. The personal expenses of all the guests were defrayed by the king with the money which he wrested from the people. With almost magical rapidity, the artificers reared cottages, stages, porticoes, for the exhibition of games, and the display of splendor scarcely equaled in the visions of Oriental romances.

The first entertainment was a tournament. The cavaliers were gorgeously dressed in the most glittering garb of the palmiest days of feudalism, magnificently mounted with wondrous trappings, with their shields and devices,

Magnificent fêtes.

with their attendant pages, equerries, heralds at arms. Among them all the king shone pre-eminent. His dress, and the housings of his charger, embellished with the crown jewels, glittered with a profusion of costly gems which no one else could equal.

The queen, with three hundred ladies of the court, brilliant in beauty, and in the most attractive dress, sat upon a platform, beneath triumphal arches, to view the procession as it passed. The gleaming armor of the cavaliers, their prancing steeds, the waving of silken banners, and the flourish of trumpets, presented a spectacle such as no one present had ever conceived of before.

The tilting did not cease till evening. Suddenly the blaze of four thousand torches illumined the scene with new brilliance. Tables were spread for a banquet, loaded with every delicacy.

" The tables were served by two hundred attendants, habited as dryads, wood deities, and fawns. Behind the tables, which were in the form of a vast crescent, an orchestra arose as if by magic. The tables were illuminated by five hundred girandoles. A gilt balustrade inclosed the whole of the immense area."

1—13

CHAPTER VI.

DEATH IN THE PALACE.

THE festivities to which we have alluded in the last chapter, the expenses of which were sufficient almost to exhaust the revenues of a kingdom, lasted seven days. The prizes awarded to the victors in the lists were very costly and magnificent. The renowned dramatist Molière accompanied the court on this occasion, to contribute to its amusement by the exhibition of his mirth-moving farces on the stage.

It was during these scenes that Louis XIV. selected Versailles as the site of the stupendous pile of buildings which was to eclipse all other palaces that had ever been reared on this globe. This magnificent structure, alike the monument of munificence in its appointments, and of infamy in the distress it imposed upon the overtaxed people, eventually swallowed up the sum of one hundred and sixty-six million of francs—thirty-three million dollars. It is to be remembered that at that day money was far more valuable, and far more difficult of acquisition than at the present time.

For seven years an army of workmen was employed on the palace, parks, and gardens. No expense was spared to carry into effect the king's designs. The park and gardens were laid out by the celebrated landscape gardener Lenôtre. The plans for the palace were furnished by the distinguished architect Mansard. Over thirty thousand soldiers were called from their garrisons to assist the swarms of ordinary workmen in digging the vast excavations and constructing the immense terraces. " It is estimated that not less than forty millions sterling—two hundred million dollars—were exhausted upon the laying out of these vast domains and the erection of this superb chateau. Such was the extraordinary vigor with which the works were pushed, that in 1685, hardly twenty-five years after its commencement, the whole was in readiness to receive its royal occupants. Here the royal family and the court resided until the Revolution of 1789. Every part of the interior as well as the exterior was ornamented with the works of the most emi· nent masters of the times."*

* Bradshaw's Guide through Paris and its Environs.

The most magnificent room in the palace,
called the grand gallery of Louis XIV., was
two hundred and forty-two feet long, thirty-
five feet broad, and forty-three feet high. The
splendors of the court of Louis XIV. may be
inferred from the fact that this vast apartment
was daily crowded with courtiers. The characteristic vanity of the king is conspicuously
developed in that he instituted an order of nobility as a reward for personal services. The
one great and only privilege of its members
was that they were permitted to wear a blue
coat embroidered with gold and silver precisely like that worn by the king, and to follow
the king in his hunting-parties and drives.

The position of Mademoiselle de la Vallière
was a very painful one. Though the austere
queen-mother was so ill in her chamber that
she could do but little to harass Louise, Madame Henrietta, who had been constrained to
receive her as one of her maids of honor, did
every thing in her power to keep her in a state
of perpetual anxiety. The courtiers generally
were hostile to her, from the partiality with
which she was openly regarded by the king.
The poor child was alone and desolate in the
court, and scarcely knew an hour of joy.

CONVENT OF VAL DE GRACE.

The queen-mother was rapidly sinking, devoured by a malady which not only caused her
extreme bodily suffering, but, from its loathsome character, affected her sensitive nature
with the most acute mental pangs. She retired to the convent of Val de Grace, where,
with ever-increasing devotion as death drew
near, she consecrated herself to works of piety
and prayer.

This vast structure is situated upon the left
bank of the Seine, and is now in the limits of
the city of Paris,

"Anne of Austria had enjoyed the rare privilege, so seldom accorded to her sex, of growing old without in any very eminent degree
losing her personal advantages. Her hands
and arms, which had always been singularly
beautiful, remained smooth and round, and
delicately white. Not a wrinkle marred the
dignity of her noble forehead. Her eyes,
which were remarkably fine, lost neither their
brightness nor their expression; and yet for
years she had been suffering physical pangs
only the more poignant from the resolution
with which she concealed them."*

The queen-mother had made the most hero-

* Louis XIV. and the Court of France, vol. ii., p. 145.

ic exertions to assume in public the appearance
of health and gayety. None but her physicians were made acquainted with the nature
of her malady.

The young queen, Maria Theresa, who appears to have been an amiable, pensive woman,
endowed with many quiet virtues, was devoted-
ly attached to the queen-mother. She clung
to her and followed her, while virtually abandoned by her royal spouse. She had no heart
for those courtly festivities where she saw others with higher fascinations command the admiration and devotion of her husband. The
queen was taken very ill with the measles. It
speaks well for Louis XIV., and should be re-
corded to his honor, that he devoted himself to
his sick wife, by day and by night, with the
most unremitting attention. The disease was
malignant in its form, and the king himself
was soon stricken down by it. For several
days it was feared that he would not live. As
he began to recover, he was removed to the
palace of St. Cloud. The annexed view repre-
sents the rear of the palace. The magnificent
saloons in front open upon the city, and from
the elevated site of the palace command a
splendid view of the region for many leagues
around.

THE PALACE OF ST. CLOUD.

This truly splendid chateau, but a few miles
from the Tuileries, had been assigned to Madame Henrietta. Here she resided with her
court, and here the king again found himself
under the same roof with Mademoiselle de la
Vallière.

In the mean time the health of the queen-
mother rapidly declined. She was fast sinking into the arms of death. The young queen,
Maria Theresa, having recovered, was unwilling to leave her suffering mother-in-law even
for an hour.

"The sufferings of Anne of Austria," writes
Miss Pardoe, " must indeed have been extreme,
when, superadded to the physical agony of
which she was so long the victim, her peculiar
fastidiousness of scent and touch are remembered. Throughout the whole of her illness
she had adopted every measure to conceal,
even from herself, the effects of her infirmity.
She constantly held in her hand a large fan of
Spanish leather, and saturated her linen with
the most powerful perfumes. Her sense of
contact was so acute and irritable that it was
with the utmost difficulty that cambric could
be found sufficiently fine for her use. Upon
one occasion, when Cardinal Mazarin was jest-

ing with her upon this defect, he told her 'that if she were damned, her eternal punishment would be sleeping in linen sheets.' "

Louis XIV. was too much engrossed with his private pleasures, his buildings, and rapidly multiplying diplomatic intrigues to pay much attention to his dying mother. It was not pleasant to him to contemplate the scenes of suffering in a sick-chamber. The gloom which was gathering around Anne of Austria was somewhat deepened by the intelligence she received of the death of her brother, Philip IV. of Spain. It was another admonition to her that she too must die. Though Philip IV. was a reserved and stately man, allowing himself in but few expressions of tenderness toward his family, Maria Theresa, in her isolation, wept bitterly over her father's death.

The ties of relationship are feeble in courts. Louis XIV. was growing increasingly ambitious of enlarging his domains and aggrandizing his power. The news of the death of the King of Spain was but a source of exultation to him. Though scrupulous in the discharge of the ceremonies of the Church, he was a stranger to any high sense of integrity or honor. In the treaty upon his marriage with Ma-

ria Theresa he had agreed to resign every
claim to any portion of the Spanish kingdom.
The death of Philip IV. left Spain in the
hands of a feeble woman. Louis XIV., upon
the plea that the five hundred thousand crowns
promised as the dower of his wife had not yet
been paid, resolved immediately to seize upon
the provinces of Flanders and Franche-Comté,
which then belonged to the Spanish crown.

Notwithstanding the queen-mother had become so exhausted, from long-continued and
agonizing bodily sufferings, that she could not
be moved from one bed to another without
fainting, still the festivities of the palace continued unintermitted. The moans of the dying queen in the darkened chamber could not
be heard amidst the music and the revelry of
the Louvre and the Tuileries. On the 5th of
January, 1666, Philip, the Duke of Orleans,
gave a magnificent ball in the palace of St.
Cloud. Louis XIV. was then in deep mourning for his father-in-law. Decorously he wore
the mourning dress of violet-colored velvet
adopted by the court; he, however, took care
so effectually to cover his mourning garments
with glittering and costly gems that the color
of the material could not be discerned.

While her children were engaged in these
revels, the queen-mother passed a sleepless
night of terrible suffering. It was apparent
to her that her dying hour was near at hand.
She was informed by her physician that her
life could be continued but a few hours longer. She called for her confessor, and requested every one else to leave the room. What
sins she confessed of heart or life are known
only to him and to God. Having obtained
such absolution as the priest could give, she
prepared to partake of the sacrament of the
Lord's Supper. Her son Philip, with Madame
his wife, were admitted to her chamber, where
the king soon joined them. The Archbishop
of Auch, accompanied by quite a retinue of
ecclesiastics, approached with the holy viaticum. The most scrupulous regard was paid
to all the punctilious ceremonials of courtly
etiquette.

When the bishop was about to administer
the oil of extreme unction, the dying queen requested an attendant very carefully to raise
the borders of her cap, lest the oil should touch
them, and give them an unpleasant odor. It
was one of the most melancholy and impressive of earthly scenes. The king, young, sensi-

tive, and easily overcome by momentary emotion, could not refrain from seeing in that sad spectacle, as in a mirror, his own inevitable lot. He fainted entirely away, and was borne senseless from the apartment.

On the morning of the 7th or 8th of January, 1666, Anne of Austria died. Her will was immediately brought from the cabinet and read. She bequeathed her *heart* to the convent of Val de Grace. It was taken from her body, cased in a costly urn, and conveyed to the convent in a carriage. The Archbishop of Auch seated himself beside the senseless relic, while the Duchess of Montpensier occupied another seat in the coach.

At 7 o'clock of the next evening the remains of the queen left the Louvre for the royal sepulchre at St. Denis. It was a gloomy winter's night. Many torches illumined the path of the procession, exhibiting to the thousands of spectators the solemn pageant of the burial. The ecclesiastics and the monks, in their gorgeous or picturesque robes, the royal sarcophagus, the sombre light of the torches, the royal coaches in funereal drapery, and the wailing requiems, now swelling upon the breeze, and now dying away, blending with the voices of tolling bells, presented one of the most mournful and instructive of earthly spectacles. The queen had passed to that tribunal where no aristocratic privileges are recognized, and where all earthly wealth and rank are disregarded.

The funeral services were prolonged and imposing. It was not until two hours after midnight that the remains were deposited in the vaults of the venerable abbey, the oldest Christian church in France.

INTERIOR OF ST. DENIS.

The death of the queen-mother does not

seem to have produced much effect upon the
conduct of her ambitious and pleasure-loving
son. He had cruelly betrayed the young and
guileless Mademoiselle de la Vallière, and she
never ceased to weep over her sad fate. The
king, however, conferred upon her the duchy
of Vaujours, and the title of Madame. Her
beauty began to fade. Younger and happier
faces attracted the king. He became more
and more arrogant and domineering.

There was at that time rising into notice in
this voluptuous court a young lady who was
not only magnificently beautiful, but extremely brilliant in her intellectual endowments.
She was of illustrious birth, and was lady of
the palace to the young queen. She deliberately fixed her affections upon Louis, and resolved to employ all the arts of personal loveliness and the fascinations of wit to win his
exclusive favor. She had given her hand,
constrained by her family, to the young Marquis de Montespan. She had, however, stated
at the time that with her hand she did not
give her heart.

The young marquis seems to have been a
very worthy man. Disgusted with the folly
and the dissipation of the court, he was anxious

to withdraw with his beautiful bride to his ample estates in Provence. She, however, entirely devoted to pleasure, and absorbed in her ambitious designs, refused to accompany him, pleading the duty she owed her royal mistress. He went alone. Madame de Montespan was thus relieved of the embarrassment of his presence.

Louis XIV., while apparently immersed in frivolous and guilty pleasures, was developing very considerable ability as a sovereign. It daily became more clearly manifest that he was not a man of pleasure merely; that he had an imperial will, and that he was endowed with unusual administrative energies.

The Duke de Mazarin, a relative and rich heir of the deceased cardinal, and who assumed an austere and cynical character, ventured on one occasion, when displeased with some act of the king, to approach him in the presence of several persons and say,

"Sire, Saint Geneviève appeared to me last night. She is much offended by the conduct of your majesty, and has foretold to me that if you do not reform your morals the greatest misfortunes will fall upon your kingdom."

The whole circle stood aghast at his effrontery. But the king, without exhibiting the slightest emotion, in slow and measured accents, replied,

" And I, Monsieur de Mazarin, have recently had several visions, by which I have been warned that the late cardinal, your uncle, plundered my people, and that it is time to make his heirs disgorge the booty. Remember this, and be persuaded that the very next time you permit yourself to offer me unsolicited advice, I shall act upon the mysterious information I have received."

The duke attempted no reply. Such developments of character effectually warded off all approaches of familiarity.

The fugitive and needy Charles II. had sold to Louis XIV., for about one million of dollars, the important commercial town of Dunkirk, in French Flanders. The king, well aware of the importance of the position, had employed thirty thousand men to fortify the place.

Louis now sent an army of thirty-five thousand men, in the highest state of military discipline, to seize the coveted Spanish provinces of Flanders and Franche-Comté. At the same time, he sent a reserve of eight thousand troops to Dunkirk. The widowed Queen of Spain,

acting as regent for her infant son, could make
no effectual resistance. She had but eight thousand troops, in small garrisons, scattered over
those provinces. The march of the French
army was but as a holiday excursion. Fortress
after fortress fell into their hands. Soon the
banners of Louis floated proudly over the whole
territory. The king displayed his sagacity by
granting promotion for services rendered rather than to birth. This inspired the army with
great ardor. He also boldly entered the trenches under fire, and exposed himself to the most
imminent peril.

The opposite side of the king's character is
displayed in the fact that he accompanied the
camp with all the ladies of his court, eighteen
in number. In each captured city, the king
and court, in magnificent banqueting-halls and
gorgeous saloons, indulged in the gayest revelry. Amidst the turmoil of the camp, these
haughty men and high-born dames surrounded themselves with the magnificence of the
Louvre and the Tuileries, and were served with
every delicacy from gold and silver plate.

The king, by the advice of his renowned
minister of war, Marshal Louvois, placed strong
garrisons in the cities he had captured, while

the celebrated engineer, M. Vauban, was intrusted with enlarging and strengthening the
fortifications. From this victorious campaign
Louis XIV. returned to Paris, receiving adulation from the courtiers as if he were more
than mortal.

Madame de Montespan accompanied the
court on this military pleasure tour. She
availed herself of every opportunity to attract
the attention of the king and ingratiate herself
in his favor. She so far succeeded in exciting
the jealousy of the queen against Madame de
la Vallière, upon whom she was at the same
time lavishing her most tender caresses, that
her majesty treated the sensitive and despond-
ing favorite with such rudeness that, with a
crushed spirit, she decided to leave the court
and retire to Versailles, there to await the conclusion of the campaign. The king, however,
interposed to prevent her departure, while at
the same time he was daily treating her with
more marked neglect, as he turned his attention
to the rival, now rapidly gaining the ascendency.
The unfortunate Louise was doomed to daily
martyrdom. She could not be blind to the fact
that the king's love was fast waning. Conscience tortured her, and she wept bitterly.

Before her there was opened only the vista of weary years of neglect and remorse.

But the Marchioness of Montespan was mingling for herself a cup of bitterness which she, in her turn, was to drain to its dregs. Her noble husband wrote most imploring letters, beseeching her to return to him with their infant child.

"Come," he wrote in one of his letters, "and take a near view, my dear Athenaïs, of these stupendous Pyrenees, whose every ravine is a landscape, and every valley an Eden. To all these beauties yours alone is wanting. You will be here like Diana, the divinity of these noble forests."

The excuses which the marchioness offered did by no means satisfy her husband. His heart was wounded and his suspicions aroused. At last he was apprised of her manifest endeavors to attract the attention of the king. He wrote severely; informed her of the extent of his knowledge. He threatened to expose her conduct to her own family, and to shut her up in a convent. At the same time, he commanded her to send to him, by the messenger who bore his letter, their little son, that he might not be contaminated by association with so unworthy a mother.

It was too late. The marchioness was involved in such guilty relations with the king
that she could not easily be extricated. Still
she was much alarmed by the angry letter of
her husband. The king perceived her anxiety,
and inquired the cause. She placed the letter
in his hands. He read it, changing color as he
read. He then coolly remarked,

"Our position is a difficult one. It requires
much precaution. I will, however, take care
that no violence shall be offered you. You had
better, however, send him your son. The child
is useless here, and perhaps inconvenient. The
marquis, deprived of the child, may be driven
to acts of severity."

A mother's love was strong in the bosom of
the marchioness. She wept aloud, and declared that she would sooner die than part with
her son. Her husband soon after came to Paris. He addressed the king in a very firm and
reproachful letter, and for three months made
earnest applications to the pope for a divorce.
But the pope, afraid of offending Louis XIV.,
turned a deaf ear to his supplications. It was
in vain for a noble, however exalted his rank,
to contend against the king.

The injured marquis, finding all his efforts

vain, returned wifeless and childless to his
chateau. Announcing that to him his wife
was dead, he assumed the deepest mourning,
draped his house and the liveries of his servants in crape, and ordered a funeral service to
take place in the parish church. A numerous
concourse attended, and all the sad ceremonies
of burial were solemnized.

The king was greatly annoyed. The scandal, which spread throughout the kingdom,
placed him in a very unenviable position. The
marquis would probably have passed the rest
of his life in one of the *oubliettes* of the Bastile had he not escaped from France. Madame
de Montespan, in her wonderfully frank Memoirs, records all these facts without any apparent consciousness of the infamy to which
they consign her memory. She even claims
the merit of protecting her injured husband
from the dungeon, saying,

" Not being naturally of a bad disposition, I
never would allow of his being sent to the Bastile."

There were continual antagonisms arising
between Madame de la Vallière and Madame
de Montespan. They were both ladies of hon-
or in the household of the queen, who, silent

and sad, and ever seeking retirement, endeavored to close her eyes to the guilty scenes transpiring around her. Sin invariably brings sorrow. The king, supremely selfish as he was,
must have been a stranger to any peace of
mind. He professed full faith in Christianity.
Even lost spirits may believe and tremble.
The precepts of Jesus were often faithfully
proclaimed from the pulpit in his hearing.
Remorse must have frequently tortured his
soul.

From these domestic tribulations he sought
relief in the vigorous prosecution of his plans
for national aggrandizement. He plunged into
diplomatic intrigues, marshaled armies, built
ships, multiplied and enlarged his sea-ports, es
tablished colonies, reared magnificent edifices,
encouraged letters, and with great sagacity
pushed all enterprises which could add to the
glory and power of France.

The king had never been on good terms with
his brother Philip. Louis was arrogant and
domineering. Philip was jealous, and not disposed obsequiously to bow the knee to his imperious brother. The king was unrelenting in
the exactions of etiquette. There were three
seats used in the presence of royalty: the arm·

chair, for members of the royal family; the folded chair, something like a camp-stool, for the highest of the nobility; and the bench, for other dignitaries who were honored with a residence at court. Philip demanded of his brother that his wife, Henrietta, the daughter of Charles I. of England, and the sister of Louis XIII., being of royal blood, should be allowed the privilege of taking an arm-chair in the saloons of the queen. The king made the following remarkable reply:

"That can not be permitted. I beg of you not to persist in such a request. It was not I who established these distinctions. They existed long before you and I were born. It is for your interest that the dignity of the crown should neither be weakened or encroached upon. If from Duke of Orleans you should one day become King of France, I know you well enough to believe that this is a point on which you would be inexorable.

"In the presence of God, you and I are two beings precisely similar to our fellow-men; but in the eyes of men we appear as something extraordinary, superior, greater, and more perfect than others. The day on which the people cast off this respect and this voluntary veneration, by which alone monarchy is upheld, they will see us only their equals, suffering from the same evils, and subject to the same weaknesses as themselves. This once accomplished, all illusion will be over. The laws, no longer sustained by a controlling power, will become black lines upon white paper. Your chair without arms and my arm-chair will be simply two pieces of furniture of equal importance."

To these forcible remarks, indicating deep reflection, the Duke of Orleans, a nobleman rioting in boundless wealth, and enjoying amazing feudal privileges, could make no reply. The coronet of the noble and the crown of the absolute king would both fall to the ground so soon as the masses of the people should escape from the thrall of ignorance and deception. Philip left his brother silenced, yet exasperated. A petty warfare was carried on between them, by which they daily became more alienated from each other.

The king, elated by his easy conquest of Flanders, resolved to seize upon Holland, and then proceed to annex to France the whole of the Low Countries. The Dutch, a maritime people, though powerful at sea, had but a feeble land force. Holland was in alliance with England. The first object of Louis was to dissolve this alliance. There were two influences, money and beauty, which were omnipotent with the contemptible Charles II. Henrietta, the wife of Philip, was sent as embassadress to the court of her brother. The whole French court escorted her to the coast. The pomp displayed on this occasion surpassed any thing which had heretofore been witnessed in France. The escort consisted of thirty thousand men in the van and the rear of the royal cortège. The most beautiful women of the court accompanied the queen. Maria Theresa, the queen, and Henrietta, occupied the same coach. The ladies of their households followed in their carriages.

The king's two favorites—Madame de la Vallière, whose beauty and power were on the wane, and Madame de Montespan, who was then in the zenith of her triumph—were often invited by the king to take a seat in the royal carriage by the side of the queen and Madame. The most beautiful woman then in the French court was Louise Rénée, subsequently known in English annals as the Duchess of Portsmouth. She was to accompany

her royal mistress to the court of Charles II.,
and had received secret instructions from the
king in reference to the influence she was to
exert. Louise Rénée was to be the bribe and
the motive power to control the king.

Brilliant as was this royal cortège, the journey, to its prominent actors, was a very sad
one. The queen, pliant and submissive as she
usually was, could not refrain from some expressions of bitterness in being forced to such
intimate companionship with her rivals in the
king's favor. There were also constant heart-
burnings and bickerings, which etiquette could
not restrain, between Philip and his spouse
Henrietta. *Madame* was going to London as
the confidential messenger of the king, and she
refused to divulge to her husband the purpose
of her visit. Louis XIV. was embarrassed by
three ladies, each of whom claimed his exclusive attention, and each of whom was angry if
he smiled upon either of the others. In such
a party there could be no happiness.

As this gorgeous procession, crowding leagues
of the road, swept along, few of the amazed
peasants who gazed upon the glittering spectacle could have suspected the misery which was
gnawing at the heart of these high-born men

and proud dames. Upon arriving at the coast, Henrietta, with her magnificent suite, embarked for England. The negotiation was perfectly successful. The fascinating Louise Rénée immediately made the entire conquest of the king. Her consent to remain a member of his court, and the offer of several millions of money to Charles II., secured his assent to whatever the French king desired. It is said that he the more readily abandoned his alliance with Holland, since he hated the Protestants there, whose religion so severely condemned his worthless character and wretched life. A treaty of alliance was speedily drawn up between Charles II. and Louis XIV.

His Britannic majesty then, with a splendid retinue, accompanied his sister Henrietta to the coast, where she embarked for Calais. The French court met her there with all honors. The return to Paris was slow. At every important town the court tarried for a season of festivities. Henrietta, or *Madame*, as the French invariably entitled her, established her court at St. Cloud. Her husband, Monsieur, was very much irritated against her. Neither of them took any pains to conceal from others their alienation.

Madame was in the ripeness of her rare beauty, and enjoyed great influence in the court.
The poor queen, Maria Theresa, was but a
cipher. She was heart-crushed, and devoted
herself to the education of her children, and
to the society of a few Spanish ladies whom
she had assembled around her. The king,
grateful for the services which Henrietta had
rendered him in England, and alike fascinated
by her loveliness and her vivacity, was lavishing upon her his constant and most marked attentions, not a little to the chagrin of her irritated and jealous husband.

On the 27th of June, 1669, Henrietta rose at
an early hour, and, after some conversation
with Madame de Lafayette, to whom she declared she was in admirable health, she attended mass, and then went to the room of her
daughter, Mademoiselle d'Orleans. She was in
glowing spirits, and enlivened the whole company by her vivacious conversation. After calling for a glass of succory water, which she
drank, she dined. The party then repaired to
the saloon of *Monsieur*. He was sitting for his
portrait. Henrietta, reclining upon a lounge,
apparently fell into a doze. Her friends were
struck with the haggard and deathly expres-

sion which her countenance suddenly assumed,
when she sprang up with cries of agony. All
were greatly alarmed. Her husband appeared
as much so as the rest. She called for another
draught of succory water. It was brought to
her in an enameled cup from which she was
accustomed to drink.

She took the cup in one hand, and then,
pressing her hand to her side in a spasm of
pain, exclaimed, "I can scarcely breathe. Take
me away—take me away! I can support myself no longer." With much difficulty she was
led to her chamber by her terrified attendants.
There she threw herself upon her bed in convulsions of agony, crying out that she was dying, and praying that her confessor might immediately be sent for. Three physicians were
speedily in attendance. Her husband entered
her chamber and kneeled at her bedside. She
threw her arms around his neck, exclaiming,

"Alas! you have long ceased to love me;
but you are unjust, for I have never wronged
you." Suddenly she raised herself upon her
elbow, and said to those weeping around her,
"I have been poisoned by the succory water
which I have drank. Probably there has been
some mistake. I am sure, however, that I have

been poisoned. Unless you wish to see me die, you must immediately administer some antidote."

Her husband did not seem at all agitated by this statement, but directed that some of the succory water should be given to a dog to ascertain its effects. Madame Desbordes, the first *femme de chambre*, who had prepared the beverage, declared that the experiment should be made upon herself. She immediately poured out a glass, and drank it.

Various antidotes for poisons were administered. They created the most deadly sickness, without changing the symptoms or alleviating the pain. It soon became evident that the princess was dying. The livid complexion, glassy eyes, and shrunken nose and lips, showed that some agent of terrific power was consuming her life. A chill perspiration oozed from her forehead, her pulse was imperceptible, and her extremities icy cold.

The king soon arrived, accompanied by the queen. Louis XIV. was greatly affected by the changed appearance and manifestly dying condition of Henrietta. He sat upon one side of the bed and *Monsieur* upon the other, both weeping bitterly. The agony of the princess

1—15

226   LOUIS XIV.   [1669

Death scene of Henrietta.   Suspicion of Louis.

was dreadful. In most imploring tones she begged that something might be done to mitigate her sufferings. The attendant physicians announced that she was dying. Extreme unction was administered, the crucifix fell from her hand, a convulsive shuddering shook her frame, and Henrietta was dead.

"Only nine hours previously, Henrietta of England had been full of life, and loveliness, and hope, the idol of a court, and the centre of the most brilliant circle in Europe. And now, as the tearful priest arose from his knees, the costly curtains of embroidered velvet were drawn around a cold, pale, motionless, and livid corpse."

A post-mortem examination revealed the presence of poison so virulent in its action that a portion of the stomach was destroyed. Dreadful suspicion rested upon her husband. The king, in a state of intense agitation, summoned his brother to his presence, and demanded that he should confess his share in the murder. Monsieur clasped in his hand the insignia of the Holy Ghost, which he wore about his neck, and took the most solemn oath that he was both directly and indirectly innocent of the death of his wife. Still the circumstantial evidence was so strong against him that he could not escape the terrible suspicion.

Notwithstanding the absolute proof that the death of the princess was caused by poison, still an official statement was soon made out, addressed to the British court, and widely promulgated, in which it was declared that the princess died of a malignant attack of bilious fever. Several physicians were bribed to sign this declaration.

Notwithstanding this statement, the king made vigorous exertions to discover the perpetrators of the crime. The following facts were soon brought to light. The king, some time before, much displeased with the Chevalier de Lorraine, a favorite and adviser of Monsieur, angrily arrested him, and imprisoned him in the Chateau d'If, a strong and renowned fortress on Marguerite Island, opposite Cannes. Here he was treated with great rigor. He was not allowed to correspond, or even to speak with any persons but those on duty within the fortress. *Monsieur* was exceedingly irritated by this despotic act. He ventured loudly to upbraid his brother, and bitterly accused *Madame* of having caused the arrest of his bosom friend, the chevalier.

Circumstances directed the very strong suspicions of the king to M. Pernon, controller of
the household of the princess, as being implicated in the murder. The king ordered him
to be secretly arrested, and brought by a back
staircase to the royal cabinet. Every attendant was dismissed, and his majesty remained
alone with the prisoner. Fixing his eyes sternly upon the countenance of M. Pernon, Louis
said, "If you reveal every circumstance relative to the death of *Madame,* I promise you
full pardon. If you are guilty of the slightest
concealment or prevarication, your life shall be
the forfeit."

The controller then confessed that the Chevalier de Lorraine had, through the hands of a
country gentleman, M. Morel, who was not at
all conscious of the nature of the commission
he was fulfilling, sent the poison to two con-
federates at St. Cloud. This package was delivered to the Marquis d'Effiat and Count de
Beuvron, intimate friends of the chevalier, and
who had no hope that he would be permitted
to return to Paris so long as *Madame* lived.
The Marquis d'Effiat contrived to enter the
closet of the princess, and rubbed the poison
on the inside of the enameled cup from which

Henrietta was invariably accustomed to drink
her favorite beverage.

The king listened intently to this statement,
pressed his forehead with his hand, and then
inquired, in tones which indicated that he was
almost afraid to put the question, "And *Monsieur*—was he aware of this foul plot?"

"No, sire," was the prompt reply. "*Monsieur* can not keep a secret; we did not venture to confide in him."

Louis appeared much relieved. After a moment's pause, he asked, with evident anxiety,
"Will you swear to this?"

"On my soul, sire," was the reply.

The king asked no more. Summoning an
officer of the household, he said, "Conduct M.
Pernon to the gate of the palace, and set him
at liberty."

Such events were so common in the courts
of feudal despotism in those days of crime,
that this atrocious murder seems to have produced but a momentary impression. Poor
Henrietta was soon forgotten. The tides of
gayety and fashion ebbed and flowed as ever
through the saloons of the royal palaces. No
one was punished. It would hardly have been
decorous for the king to hang men for the mur-

der of the princess, when he had solemnly announced that she had died of a bilious fever.
The Chevalier de Lorraine was ere long recalled to court. There he lived in unbridled
profligacy, enjoying an annual income of one
hundred thousand crowns, till death summoned
him to a tribunal where neither wealth nor
rank can purchase exemption from crime.

Henrietta, who was but twenty-six years of
age at the time of her death, left two daughters, but no son. *Monsieur* soon dried his tears.
He sought a new marriage with his rich, renowned cousin, the Duchess of Montpensier.
But she declined his offered hand. With inconceivable caprice, she was fixing her affections upon a worthless adventurer, a miserable
coxcomb, the Duke de Lauzun, who was then
disgracing by his presence the court of the
Louvre. This singular freak, an additional evidence that there is no accounting for the va-
garies of love, astonished all the courts of Europe. *Monsieur* then turned to the Princess
Charlotte Elizabeth of Bavaria. The alliance
was one dictated by state policy. *Monsieur*
reluctantly assented to it under the moral com-
pulsion of the king. The advent of this most
eccentric of women at the French court created

general astonishment and almost consternation.
She despised etiquette, and dressed in the most
outrè fashion, while she displayed energies of
mind and sharpness of tongue which brought
all in awe of her. The following is the portrait which this princess, eighteen years of age,
has drawn of herself:

" I was born in Heidelberg in 1652. I must
necessarily be ugly, for I have no features,
small eyes, a short, thick nose, and long, flat
lips. Such a combination as this can not produce a physiognomy. I have heavy hanging
cheeks and a large face, and nevertheless am
short and thick. To sum up all, I am an ugly
little object. If I had not a good heart, I
should not be bearable any where. To ascertain if my eyes have any expression, it would
be necessary to examine them with a micro-
scope. There could not probably be found on
earth hands more hideous than mine. The
king has often remarked it to me, and made
me laugh heartily. Not being able with any
conscience to flatter myself that I possessed
any thing good looking, I have made up my
mind to laugh at my own ugliness. I have
found the plan very successful, and frequently
discover plenty to laugh at."

Notwithstanding the princess was ready to speak of herself in these terms of ridicule, she was by no means disposed to grant the same privilege to others. She was a woman of keen observation, and was ever ready to resent any offense with the most sarcastic retaliation. She perceived very clearly the sensation which her presence, and the manners which she had very deliberately chosen to adopt, had excited. Madame de Fienne was one of the most brilliant wits of the court. She ventured to make herself and others merry over the oddities of the newly-arrived Duchess of Orleans, in whose court both herself and her husband were pensioners. The duchess took her by the hand, led her aside, and, riveting upon her her unquailing eye, said, in slow and emphatic tones,

"Madame, you are very amiable and very witty. You possess a style of conversation which is endured by the king and by *Monsieur* because they are accustomed to it; but I, who am only a recent arrival at the court, am less familiar with its spirit. I forewarn you that I become incensed when I am made a subject of ridicule. For this reason, I was anxious to give you a slight warning. If you spare me, we shall get on very well together;

but if, on the contrary, you treat me as you
do others, I shall say nothing to yourself, but I
shall complain to your husband, and if he does
not correct you, I shall dismiss him."

The hint was sufficient. Neither Madame
de Fienne nor any other lady of the court ventured after this to utter a word of witticism on
the subject of the Duchess of Orleans.

Chapter VII.

The War in Holland.

MADAME DE MONTESPAN was now the reigning favorite. The conscience-stricken king could not endure to think of death. He studiedly excluded from observation every thing which could remind him of that doom of mortals. All the badges of mourning were speedily laid aside, and efforts were made to banish from the court the memory of the young and beautiful Princess Henrietta, whose poisoned body was mouldering to dust in the tomb.

The king had a childish fondness for brilliant gems. In his cabinet he had a massive and costly secretary of elaborately carved rosewood. Upon its shelves he had arrayed the crown jewels, which he often handled and examined with the same delight with which a miser counts his gold.

Mademoiselle de Montpensier, in her interesting Memoirs, relates the following anecdote, which throws interesting light upon the char-

acter of the king at this time. It will be re
membered that Louis XIV. was born in one of
the palaces at St. Germain, about fifteen miles
from Paris. The magnificent terrace on the
left bank of the winding Seine commands perhaps as enchanting a view as can be found any
where in this world. The domes and towers
of Paris appear far away in the north. The
wide, luxuriant valley of the Seine, studded
with villages and imposing castles, lies spread
out in beautiful panorama before the eye. The
king had expended between one and two millions of dollars in embellishing the royal resi-
dences here. But as the conscience of the king
became more sensitive, and repeated deaths
forced upon him the conviction that he too
must eventually die, St. Germain not only lost
all its charms, but became a place obnoxious to
him. From the terrace there could be dis-
tinctly seen, a few leagues to the east, the tower
and spire of St. Denis, the burial-place of the
kings of France. To Louis it suddenly became
as torturing a sight as to have had his coffin
ostentatiously displayed in his banqueting-hall.

When Anne of Austria was lying on her bed
of suffering, the king was one day pacing alone
the terrace of St. Germain. Dark clouds were

ST. DENIS.

drifting through the sky.   One of these clouds
seemed to gather over the towers of St. Denis.
To the excited imagination of the king, the
vapor wreathed itself into the form of a hearse,
surmounted by the arms of Austria.   In a few
days the king followed the remains of his mother to the dark vaults of this their last resting-
place.   Just before the death of the hapless
Henrietta, the same gloomy towers appeared
to the king in a dream enveloped in flames,

and in the midst of the fire there was a skeleton holding in his hand a lady's rich jewelry.
But a few days after this the king was constrained to follow the remains of the beauti
ful Henrietta to this sepulchre. God seems to
have sent warning upon warning upon this
wicked king. Absorbed in ambitious plans
and guilty passions, Louis had but little time
or thought to give to his neglected wife or her
children. In the same year his two daughters
died, and with all the pageantry of royal woe
they were also entombed at St. Denis.

It is not strange that, under these circumstances, the king, to whom the Gospel of Christ
was often faithfully preached, and who was living in the most gross violation of the principles
of the religion of Jesus, should have recoiled
from a view of those towers, which were ever a
reminder to him of death and the grave. He
could no longer endure the palace at St. Germain. The magnificent panorama of the city,
the winding Seine, the flowery meadows, the
forest, the villages, and the battlemented cha-
teaux lost all their charms, since the towers of
St. Denis would resistlessly arrest his eye, for-
cing upon his soul reflections from which he instinctively recoiled. He therefore abandoned

St. Germain entirely, and determined that the palace he was constructing at Versailles should be so magnificent as to throw every other abode of royalty into the shade.

Madame de la Vallière was daily becoming more wretched. Fully conscious of her sin and shame, deserted by the king, supplanted by a new favorite, and still passionately attached to her royal betrayer, she could not restrain that grief which rapidly marred her beauty. The waning of her charms, and the reproaches of her silent woe, increasingly repelled the king from seeking her society. One day Louis entered the apartment of Louise, and found her weeping bitterly. In cold, reproachful tones, he demanded the cause of her uncontrollable grief. The poor victim, upon the impulse of the moment, gave vent to all the gushing anguish of her soul — her sense of guilt in the sight of God—her misery in view of her ignominious position, and her brokenness of heart in the consciousness that she had lost the love of one for whom she had periled her very soul.

The king listened impatiently, and then haughtily replied, " Let there be an end to this. I love you, and you know it. But I am not to be constrained." He reproached her for

her obstinacy in refusing the friendship of her
rival, Madame de Montespan, and added the
cutting words, "You have needed, as well as
Madame de Montespan, the forbearance and
countenance of your sex."

Poor Louise was utterly crushed. She had
long been thinking of retiring to a convent.
Her decision was now formed. She devoted
a few sad days to the necessary arrangements,
took an agonizing leave, as she supposed forever, of her children, to whom she was tenderly attached, and for whom the king had made
ample provision, and, addressing a parting letter to him, entered her carriage, to seek, for a
second time, a final retreat in the convent of
Chaillot.

It was late in the evening when she entered
those gloomy cells where broken hearts find a
living burial. To the abbess she said, "I have
no longer a home in the palace; may I hope
to find one in the cloister?" The abbess received her with true Christian sympathy. After listening with a tearful eye to the recital of
her sorrows, she conducted her to the cell in
which she was to pass the night.

"She could not pray, although she cast herself upon her knees beside the narrow pallet,

and strove to rejoice that she had at length escaped from the trials of a world which had
wearied her, and of which she herself was
weary. There was no peace, no joy in her
rebel heart. She thought of the first days of
her happiness; of her children, who on the
morrow would ask for her in vain; and then,
as memory swept over her throbbing brain, she
remembered her former flight to Chaillot, and
that it was the king himself who had led her
back again into the world. Her brow burned
as the question forced itself upon her, Would
he do so a second time? would he once more
hasten, as he had then done, to rescue her from
the living death to which she had consigned
herself as an atonement for her past errors?

"But hour after hour went by, and all was silent. Hope died within her. Daylight streamed dimly into the narrow casement of her cell.
Soon the measured step of the abbess fell upon
her ear as she advanced up the long gallery,
striking upon the door of each cell as she approached, and uttering in a solemn voice, 'Let
us bless the Lord.' To which appeal each of the
sisters replied in turn, 'I give him thanks.'"

The deceptive heart of Louise led her to
hope, notwithstanding she had voluntarily

sought the cloister, that the king, yearning for her presence, would come himself, as soon as he heard of her departure, and affectionately force her back to the Louvre. Early in the morning she heard the sound of carriage-wheels entering the court-yard of the convent. Her heart throbbed with excitement. Soon she was summoned from her cell to the parlor. Much to her disappointment, the king was not there, but his minister, M. Colbert, presented to her a very affectionate letter from his majesty urging her return. As she hesitated, M. Colbert pleaded earnestly in behalf of his sovereign.

The feeble will of Louise yielded, while yet she blushed at her own weakness. Tears filled her eyes as she took leave of the abbess, grasping her hand, and saying, "This is not a farewell; I shall assuredly return, and perhaps very soon." The king was much moved in receiving her, and, with great apparent cordiality, thanked her for having complied with his entreaties. Even the heart of Madame de Montespan was touched. She received with words of love and sympathy the returned fugitive, whose rivalry she no longer feared, and in

1—16

whose sad career she perhaps saw mirrored her own future doom.

Madame de Montespan was then in the ze-nith of her power. The king had assigned her the beautiful chateau of Clagny, but a short distance from Versailles. Here she lived in great splendor, entertaining foreign embassa-dors, receiving from them costly gifts, and in-troducing them to her children as if they were really princes of the blood.

Notwithstanding the corruptions of the pa-pal Church, there were in that Church many faithful ministers of Jesus Christ. Some of them, in their preaching, inveighed very se-verely against the sinful practices in the court. Not only Madame de Montespan, but the king, often knew that they were directly referred to. But the guilty yet sagacious monarch care-fully avoided any appropriation of the denun-ciations to himself. Still, he was so much an-noyed that he seriously contemplated urging Madame de Montespan to retire to a convent. He even authorized the venerable Bossuet, then Bishop of Condom, to call upon Madame de Montespan, and suggest in his name that she should withdraw from the court and retire to the seclusion of the cloister. But the haughty favorite, conscious of the power of her charms, and knowing full well that the king had only submitted to the suggestion, peremptorily refused. She judged correctly. The king was well pleased to have her remain.

The preparations which the king was making for the invasion of Holland greatly alarmed the Dutch government. France had become powerful far beyond any other Continental kingdom. The king had the finest army in Europe. Turenne, Condé, Vauban, ranked among the ablest generals and engineers of any age. While Louis XIV. was apparently absorbed in his pleasures, Europe was surprised to see vast trains of artillery and ammunition wagons crowding the roads of his northern provinces. In his previous campaign, Louis had taken Flanders in three months, and Franche-Comté in three weeks. These rapid conquests had alarmed neighboring nations, and Holland, Switzerland, and England had entered into an alliance to resist farther encroachments, should they be attempted.

Louis affected to be very angry that such a feeble state as Holland should have the impudence to think of limiting his conquests. Having, as we have mentioned, detached England

from the alliance by bribing with gold and female charms the miserable Charles II., Louis
was ready, without any declaration of war, even
without any *openly avowed* cause of grievance,
to invade Holland, and annex the territory to
his realms. The States-General, alarmed in
view of the magnitude of the military operations which were being made upon their borders, sent embassadors to the French court humbly to inquire if these preparations were de-
signed against Holland, the ancient and faithful ally of France, and, if so, in what respect
Holland had offended.

Louis XIV. haughtily and insolently replied,
" I shall make use of my troops as my own dignity renders advisable. I am not responsible
for my conduct to any power whatever."

The real ability of the king was shown in
the effectual measures he adopted to secure,
without the chance of failure, the triumphant
execution of his plans. Twenty millions of
people had been robbed of their hard earnings
to fill his army chests with gold. An army of
a hundred and thirty thousand men, in the
highest state of discipline, and abundantly sup-
plied with all the munitions of war, were on
the march for the northern frontiers of France.

These troops were supported by a combined English and French fleet of one hundred and thirty vessels of war. It was the most resist-less force, all things considered, Europe had then ever witnessed. We shall not enter into the details of this campaign, which are inter-esting only to military men. Twelve hundred of the sons of the nobles were organized into a body-guard, ever to surround the king. They were decorated with the most brilliant uni-forms, glittering with embroideries of gold and silver, and were magnificently mounted. The terrible bayonet was then, for the first time, at-tached to the musket. Light pontoons of brass for crossing the rivers were carried on wagons. A celebrated writer, M. Pelisson, accompanied the king, to give a glowing narrative of his achievements.

As there had been no declaration of war and no commencement of hostilities, the king pur-chased a large amount of military stores even in the states of Holland, which, no one could doubt, he was preparing to invade. A Dutch merchant, being censured by Prince Maurice for entering into a traffic so unpatriotic, replied,

"My lord, if there could be opened to me by sea any advantageous commerce with the in-

fernal regions, I should certainly go there, even
at the risk of burning my sails."

Louis made arrangements that money should
be liberally expended to bribe the command-
ants of the Dutch fortresses. To oppose all
these moral and physical forces, Holland had
but twenty-five thousand soldiers, poorly armed
and disciplined. They were under the command of the Prince of Orange, who was in
feeble health, and but twenty-two years of age.
But this young prince proved to be one of the
most extraordinary men of whom history gives
any account; yet it was manifestly impossible
for him now to arrest the torrent about to invade his courts.

Louis rapidly pushed his troops forward into
the unprotected states of Holland which bor-
dered the left banks of the Rhine. His march
was unresisted. Liberally he paid for whatever he took, distributed presents to the nobles,
and, preparing to cross the river, placed his
troops in strong detachments in villages scattered along the banks of the stream. The king
himself was at the head of a choice body of
thirty thousand troops. Marshal Turenne commanded under him.

The whole country on the left bank of the

Rhine was soon in possession of the French, as
village after village fell into their hands. The
main object of the Prince of Orange was to
prevent the French from crossing the river.
Louis intended to have crossed by his pontoons,
suddenly moving upon some unexpected point.
But there came just then a very severe drouth.
The water fell so low that there was a portion
of the stream which could be nearly forded.
It would be necessary to swim the horses but
about twenty feet. The current was slow, and
the passage could be easily effected. By moving rapidly, the Prince of Orange would not
be able to collect at that point sufficient troops
seriously to embarrass the operation.

Fifteen thousand horsemen were here sent
across, defended by artillery on the banks, and
aided by boats of brass. But one man in the
French army, the young Duke de Longueville,
was killed. He lost his life through inebria-
tion, and its consequent folly and crime. Half
crazed with wine, he refused quarter to a Dutch
officer who had thrown down his arms and surrendered. Reeling in his saddle, he shot down
the officer, exclaiming, "No quarter for these
rascals." Some of the Dutch infantry, who
were just surrendering, in despair opened fire,

and the drunken duke received the death-blow he merited.

This passage of the Rhine was considered a very brilliant achievement, and added much to the military reputation of Louis XIV., though it appears to have been exclusively the feat of the Prince of Condé. The cities of Holland fell in such rapid succession into the power of the French, that scarcely an hour of the day passed in which the king did not receive the news of some conquest. An officer named Mazel sent an aid to Marshal Turenne to say,

" If you will be kind enough to send me fifty horsemen, I shall with them be able to take two or three places."

It was on the 12th of June, 1672, that the passage of the Rhine was effected. On the 20th the French king made his triumphal entrance into the city of Utrecht. The king was a Catholic—a bigoted Catholic. Corrupt as he was in life, regardless as he was in his private conduct of the precepts of Jesus, he was extremely zealous to invest the Catholic Church with power and splendor. It was with him a prominent object to give the Catholic religion the supremacy.

Amsterdam was the capital of the republic.

The capture of that city would complete the conquest. Not only the republic would perish, but Holland would, as it were, disappear from the earth, her territory being absorbed in that of France. The consternation in the metropolis was great. The most noble and wealthy families were preparing for a rapid flight to the north. Amsterdam was then the most opulent and influential commercial town in Europe. It contained a population of two hundred thousand sagacious, energetic, thrifty people. As is invariably the case in days of disaster, there were discordant counsels and angry divisions among the bewildered defenders of the imperiled realm. Some were for fiercely pressing the war, others for humbly imploring peace.

At length four deputies were sent to the French camp to intercede for the clemency of the conqueror. They were received with raillery and insult. After contemptuously compelling the deputation several times to come and go without any result, the king at last condescended to present the following as his terms:

He demanded that the States of Holland should surrender to him the whole of the ter-

ritory on the left bank of the Rhine; that they
should place in his hands, to be garrisoned by
French troops, the most important forts and fortified towns of the republic; that they should
pay him twenty millions of francs, a sum equal
to several times that amount at the present day;
that the French should be placed in command
of all the important entrances to Holland, both
by sea and land, and should be exempted from
paying any duty upon the goods they should
enter; that the Catholic religion should be established every where through the realm; and
that every year the republic should send to
Louis XIV. an embassador, with a golden med-
al, upon which there should be impressed the
declaration that the republic held all its privileges through the favor of Louis XIV. To
these conditions were to be added such as the
States-General should be compelled to make
with the other allies engaged in the war.

The nations of Europe have been guilty of
many outrages, but perhaps it would be difficult to find one more atrocious than this. In
reference to the cause of the war, Voltaire very
truly remarks, "It is a singular fact, and worthy of record, that of all the enemies, there was
not one that could allege any pretext whatever

for the war." It was an enterprise very similar to that of the coalition of Louis XII., the
Emperor Maximilian, and Spain, who conspired
for the overthrow of the Venetian republic simply because that republic was rich and prosperous.

These terms, dictated by the insolence of the
conqueror, were quite intolerable. They inspired the courage of despair. The resolution
was at once formed to perish, if perish they
must, with their arms in their hands. The
Prince of Orange had always urged the vigorous prosecution of the war. Guided by his energetic counsel, they pierced the dikes, which
alone protected their country from the waters
of the sea. The flood rushed in through the
opened barriers, converting hundreds of leagues
of fertile fields into an ocean. The inundation
flooded the houses, swept away the roads, destroyed the harvest, drowned the flocks ; and
yet no one uttered a murmur. Louis XIV.,
by his infamous demands, had united all hearts
in the most determined resistance. Amsterdam appeared like a large fortress rising in the
midst of the ocean, surrounded by ships of war,
which found depth of water to float where
ships had never floated before. The distress

was dreadful. It was the briny ocean whose waves were now sweeping over the land. It was so difficult to obtain any fresh water that it was sold for six cents a pint.

Maritime Holland, though weak upon the land, was still powerful on the sea. The united fleet of the allies did not exceed that of the republic. The Dutch Admiral Ruyter, with a hundred vessels of war and fifty fire-ships, repaired to the coasts of England in search of his foes. He met the allied fleet on the 7th of June, 1672, and in the heroic naval battle of Solbaie disabled and dispersed it. This gave Holland the entire supremacy on the sea. Thus suddenly Louis XIV. found himself checked, and no farther progress was possible.

The Prince of Orange gave all his private revenues to the state, and entered into negotiations with other powers, who were already alarmed by the encroachments of the French king. The Emperor of Germany, the Spanish court, and Flanders, entered into an alliance with the heroic prince. He even compelled Charles II. to withdraw from that union with Louis XIV. which was opposed to the interests of England, and into which his court had been reluctantly dragged. Troops from all quarters

were hurrying forward for the protection of
Holland.

The villainy of Louis XIV. was thwarted.
Chagrined at seeing his conquest at an end,
but probably with no compunctions of conscience for the vast amount of misery his crime
had caused, he left his discomfited army under
the command of Turenne and the other generals, and returned to his palaces in France.

The troops which remained in Holland com-
mitted outrages which rendered the very name
of the French detested. Louis, from the midst
of the pomp and pleasure of his palaces, still
displayed extraordinary energies. Agents were
dispatched to all the courts of Europe with
large sums of money for purposes of bribery.
By his diplomatic cunning, Hungary was roused
against Austria. Gold was lavished upon the
King of England to induce him, notwithstanding the opposition of the British Parliament,
to continue in alliance with France. Several
of the petty states of Germany were bought
over. Louis greatly increased his naval force.
He soon had forty ships of war afloat, besides
a large number of fire-ships.

But Europe had been so alarmed by his encroachments and his menaces that, notwith-

Arch of triumph.

standing his efforts at diplomacy **and intrigue,**
he was compelled to abandon his enterprise,
and withdraw his troops from the provinces he
had overrun.

In the early part of his campaign, Louis,
flushed with victory and assured of entire success, had commenced building, as a monument
of his great achievement, the arch of triumph
at the gate of St. Denis. The structure was
scarcely completed ere he was compelled to
withdraw his troops from Holland, to meet the

PORTE ST. DENIS.

foes who were crowding upon him from all
directions.

Louis XIV. now found nearly all Europe
against him. He sent twenty thousand men,
under Marshal Turenne, to encounter the forces
of the Emperor of Germany. The Prince de
Condé was sent with forty thousand troops to
assail the redoubtable Prince of Orange. Another strong detachment was dispatched to the
frontiers of Spain, to arrest the advance of the
Spanish troops. A fleet was also sent, convey-
ing a large land force, to make a diversion by
attacking the Spanish sea-ports.

Turenne, in defending the frontiers of the
Rhine, acquired reputation which has made
his name one of the most renowned in military annals. The emperor sent seventy thousand
men against him. Turenne had but twenty
thousand to meet them. By wonderful combinations, he defeated and dispersed the whole
imperial army. It added not a little to the
celebrity of Turenne that he had achieved his
victory by following his own judgment, in di
rect opposition to reiterated orders from the
minister of war, given in the name of the king.

Turenne, a merciless warrior, allowed no
considerations of humanity to interfere with

his military operations. The Palatinate, a
country on both sides the Rhine, embracing a
territory of about sixteen hundred square miles,
and a population of over three hundred thousand, was laid in ashes by his command. It
was a beautiful region, very fertile, and covered with villages and opulent cities. The Elector Palatine saw from the towers of his castle
at Manheim two cities and twenty-five villages
at the same time in flames. This awful destruction was perpetrated upon the defenseless
inhabitants, that the armies of the emperor,
encountering entire desolation, might be deprived of subsistence. It was nothing to Turenne that thousands of women and children
should be cast houseless into the fields to starve.

Alsace, with nearly a million of inhabitants,
encountered the same doom. Another province, Lorraine, which covered an area of about
ten thousand square miles, and contained a
population of one and a half millions, was
swept of all its provisions by the cavalry of
the French commander. In reference to these
military operations, Voltaire writes,

"All the injuries he inflicted seemed to be
necessary. Besides, the army of seventy thousand Germans, whom he thus prevented from

entering France, would have inflicted much
more injury than Turenne inflicted upon Lorraine, Alsace, and the Palatinate."

On the 27th of June, 1675, a cannon ball
struck Turenne, and closed in an instant his
earthly career. His renown filled Europe.
He was a successful warrior, a dissolute man;
and few who have ever lived have caused more
widespread misery than could be charged to
his account. Such is not the character which
best prepares one to stand before the judgment seat of Christ.

The war continued for two years with somewhat varying fortune, but with unvarying blood
and misery. At last peace was made on the
14th of August, 1678—the peace of Nimeguen,
as it is styled. Louis XIV. dictated the terms.
He was now at the height of his grandeur.
He had enlarged his domains by the addition
of Franche-Comté, Dunkirk, and half of Flanders. His courtiers worshiped him as a demi-
god. The French court conferred upon him,
with imposing solemnities, the title of *Louis
le Grand*. The ambition of Louis was by no
means satiated. He availed himself of the
short peace which ensued to form plans and
gather resources for new conquests

1—17

Let us now return from fields of blood to life in the palace. Madame de la Vallière, upon her return from the convent, soon found herself utterly miserable. She had hoped that reviving affection had been the inducement which led Louis to recall her. Instead of this, his attentions daily diminished. Madame de Montespan had accompanied the king in his brief trip to Holland, and returned with him to Paris. She was all-powerful at court, and seemed to delight, by word and deed, to add to the anguish of her vanquished rival. After a dreary year of wretchedness, Louise could endure no longer a residence in the palace. Her mother, who had been exceedingly distressed in view of the ignominious position occupied by her daughter, entreated her to retire to the Duchy of Vaujours with her children. Her mother promised to accompany her to that quiet yet beautiful retreat. But the spirit of Louise was broken. She longed only to sever herself entirely from the world, and to seek a living burial in the glooms of the cloister. In those days of sorrow, penitence and the spirit of devotion sprang up in her weary heart.

Louise was still young and beautiful. Her

Takes leave of her children and the queen.

passionate love for the king still held strong
dominion over her. Grief brought on a long
and dangerous illness. For many days her
life was in danger. In view of the approaching judgment, where she felt that she soon
must stand, the greatness of her transgression
harrowed her soul, and increased her desire to
spend the rest of her life in works of piety and
in prayer. When convalescent, the king con-
sented to her retirement to the Carmelite convent. Like one in a dream, she took leave of
her children without a tear. Then, entering
the apartment of the queen, she threw herself
upon her knees, and with the sobbings of a re-
morseful and despairing heart implored her
pardon for all the sorrow she had caused her.
The generous Maria Theresa raised her up,
embraced her, and declared her entirely for-
given.

The morning of her departure arrived. The
king, who was that day to leave Paris to visit
the army in Flanders, attended high mass.
Louise also attended. Absorbed in prayer,
she did not raise her eyes during the service.
She then, pale as death, and leaning upon the
arm of her mother, but for whose support she
must have fallen, advanced to take leave of

the king. The selfish monarch, with a dry eye
and a firm voice, bade her adieu, coldly expressing the hope that she would be happy in
her retreat. Without the slightest apparent
emotion, he saw Louise, with her earthly happiness utterly wrecked, enter her carriage and
drive away, to pass the remainder of her joyless years in the gloomy cell of the convent.
He then turned and conversed with his companions with as much composure as if nothing
unusual had happened.

Louise, upon her arrival at the convent, cast
herself upon her knees before the abbess, saying that hitherto she had made so ill a use of
her free will that she came to resign it to the
abbess forever. For thirty-six years the heart-
broken penitent endured the hardships of her
convent life—its narrow pallet, its hard fare,
its prolonged devotions, its silence, and its rigid
fastings. Under the name of Louisa of Mercy
she with the most exemplary fidelity performed
all her dreary duties, until, in her sixty-sixth
year, she fell asleep, and passed away, we trust,
to the bosom of that Savior who is ever ready
to receive the returning penitent.

The hapless Henrietta, duchess of Orleans,
left a very beautiful daughter, Maria Louisa.

Her charms of countenance, person, and manners attracted the admiration of the whole
court, where she was a universal favorite. She
was compelled by the king, as a matter of state
policy, to marry Charles II., the young King
of Spain, for whom she felt no affection. Bitterly she wept in view of the terrible sacrifice
she was compelled to make. But the will of
the king was inexorable. Her melancholy marriage was solemnized with much splendor in
the great chapel at St. Germain. She then
left, with undisguised reluctance, for Madrid.
The King of Spain, feeble in body, more feeble
in mind, moody and melancholy, was charmed
by her youth and beauty. Her mental endowments were such that she soon acquired entire
ascendency over him. He became pliant as
wax in her hands.

The cabinet at Vienna were alarmed lest
Maria Louisa should influence her husband to
unite with France against Germany. The
Countess de Soissons was sent as a secret agent
to the Spanish court. Beautiful and fascinating, she soon became exceedingly intimate with
the queen. One day Maria Louisa, oppressed
by the heat, expressed regret at the scarcity of
milk in Madrid, saying how much she should

enjoy a good draught. The countess assured
her that she knew where to obtain some of ex-
cellent quality, and that, with her majesty's permission, she would have it iced and present it
with her own hands. The queen received the
cup with a smile, and drank it at once. In half
an hour she was taken ill. After a few hours
of horrible agony, such as her unhappy mother
had previously endured from the same cause,
she died. In the confusion, the countess escaped from the capital. She was pursued, but
her arrangements for escape had been so skillfully made that she could not be overtaken.

Maria Theresa, the neglected queen of France,
had borne six children; but of these, at this period, there was but one surviving son, the dauphin. In his character there appeared a combination of most singular anomalies and con-
tradictions. Though exceedingly impulsive
and obstinate in obeying every freak of his
fancy, he seemed incapable of any affection,
and alike incapable of any hostility, except that
which flashed up for the moment.

"The example of his guardians had inspired
him with a few amiable qualities, but his natural vices defied eradication. His constitution-
al tendencies were all evil. His greatest pleas-

ure consisted in annoying those about him. Those who were most conversant with his humor could never guess the temper of his mind. He laughed the loudest and affected the greatest amiability when he was most exasperated, and scowled defiance when he was perfectly unruffled. His only talent was a keen sense of the ridiculous. Nothing escaped him that could be tortured into sarcasm, although no one could have guessed, from his abstracted and careless demeanor, that he was conscious of any thing that was taking place in his presence. His indolence was extreme, and his favorite amusement was lying stretched upon a sofa tapping the points of his shoes with a cane. Never, to the day of his death, had even his most intimate associates heard him express an opinion upon any subject relating to art, literature, or politics."*

Such was the imbecile young man who, by the absurd law of hereditary descent, was the destined heir to the throne of more than twenty millions of people. The king was anxious to obtain for his son a bride whose alliance would strengthen him against his enemies. With that policy alone influencing him, he ap-

* Louis XIV. and the Court of France, vol. ii., p. 268.

plied for the hand of the Princess Mary Ann
of Bavaria. It so chanced that she was in
personal appearance exceedingly unattractive.
The king said that, "though she was not handsome, he still hoped that Monseigneur would
be able to live happily with her."

The dauphin, or Monseigneur as he was called, seemed to be perfectly indifferent to the
whole matter. He at one time inquired if the
princess were free from any deformity. Upon
being told that she was, he seemed quite con-
tented, and asked no farther questions. In an-
ticipation of the marriage, a lady, Madame de
Maintenon, whose name henceforth became in-
separably connected with that of Louis XIV.,
was appointed to the distinguished post of
"mistress of the robes" to the dauphiness. We
must now introduce this distinguished lady to
our readers.

The Marchioness Françoise d'Aubigné was
born of a noble Protestant family, in the year
1635, in the prison of Niort. Her mother, with
her little boy, had been permitted to join her
imprisoned husband in his captivity. Here
Françoise was born, amidst scenes of the most
extreme poverty and misery. The emaciate
mother was unable to afford sustenance to her

infant. A sister of Baron d'Aubigné, Madame
de Vilette, took Françoise to her home at the
Chateau de Marcey, where she passed her infancy.   After an imprisonment of four years,
the baron was released; but, as he refused to
abjure Calvinism, Cardinal Richelieu would
not permit him to remain in France. He consequently, with his family, embarked for Martinique. During the passage, Françoise was
taken ill and apparently died. As one of the
crew was about to consign the body to its ocean
burial, the grief-stricken mother implored the
privilege of one parting embrace. As she
pressed the child to her heart, she perceived indications of life. The babe recovered, to occupy a position which filled the world with
her renown.

Upon the island of Martinique prosperity
smiled upon them. Madame d'Aubigné was
a Catholic, though her husband was a Protestant. She at length took ship for France,
hoping to save some portion of her husband's
sequestered estates, but was unsuccessful.
Upon her return to Martinique, she found that
Baron d'Aubigné, during her absence, deprived
of her restraining influence, had utterly ruined
himself by gambling. Overwhelmed by re

gret and misery, he almost immediately sank into the grave. Madame d'Aubigné and her two children, in the extreme of poverty, returned to France. Madame de Vilette again took the little Françoise to the chateau of Marcey As her mother was a Catholic, Françoise had been baptized by a Romish priest, and reared in the faith of her mother. The Countess de Neuillant, who was attached to the household of Anne of Austria, was her godmother, and a very intense Catholic; but Madame de Vilette, the sister of the child's father, was a Protestant. The susceptible child was soon led to adopt the faith of her protectress.

Catholic zeal was such in those days that Madame de Neuillant obtained an order from the court to remove the little girl from the Protestant family, and to place her under her own guardianship. Here every effort was made to induce Françoise to return to the Catholic faith, but neither threats nor entreaties were of any avail. She remained firm in her Protestant principles. The persecution she endured amounted almost to martyrdom. Madame de Neuillant, in her rage, imposed upon her the most humiliating and onerous domestic services. She was the servant of the

servants. She fed the horses. She suffered
from cold and hunger. Thus she, who subsequently caused the revocation of the Edict of
Nantes, and thus exposed the Protestants to
the most dreadful sufferings, was a martyr of
the religion of which she later became so terrible a scourge.

The mother, witnessing the distress of her
child, succeeded in withdrawing her from Madame de Neuillant, and placing her in a convent. Here the Ursuline nuns won her over
to the Catholic faith. Proud of their convert,
who was remarkably intelligent and attractive,
they kept her for a year. But as neither Madame de Neuillant, from whom she had been
removed, nor Madame de Vilette, who dreaded her return to Romanism, would pay her
board, they refused to give her any longer a
shelter. Françoise left the convent, and joined her mother only in time to see her sink in
sorrow to the grave. She was thus left, at
fourteen years of age, in utter destitution, dependent upon charity for support.

CHAPTER VIII.

MADAME DE MAINTENON.

THE extreme distress and destitution of
Françoise touched the heart of Madame
de Neuillant. She again took the orphan child
under her charge and returned her to school
in the convent. Françoise gradually developed remarkable beauty and intelligence. Her
quiet, unobtrusive, instinctive tact gave her
fascinating power over most who approached
her. She often visited the countess, where she
attracted much admiration from the fashionable guests who were ever assembled in her saloons. The dissolute courtiers were lavish in
their attentions to the highly-endowed child.
Established principles of virtue alone saved
her from ruin. Misfortune and sorrow had
rendered her precocious beyond her years. It
was her only and her earnest desire to take
the veil, and join the sisters in the convent
But money was needed for that purpose, and
she had none.

There was residing very near Madame de

Neuillant, a very remarkable man, Paul Scarron. He was born of a good family, and had traveled extensively. Having run through the disgraceful round of fashionable dissipation, he had become crippled by the paralysis of his lower limbs, and was living a literary life in the enjoyment of a competence. He was still young. Imperturbable gayety, wonderful conversational powers, and celebrity as a poet, caused his saloons to be crowded with distinguished and admiring friends. Some one mentioned to him the situation of Françoise d'Aubigné, and her desire to enter the convent. His kindly heart was touched, and, heading a subscription-list, he soon obtained sufficient funds from among his friends to enable her to secure the retreat she desired.

Quite overjoyed, the maiden hastened to the apartments of the poet to express her gratitude. Scarron was astonished when the apparition of a beautiful girl of fifteen, full of life, and with a figure whose symmetric grace the sculptor could with difficulty rival, appeared before him. Her heart was glowing with gratitude which her lips could hardly express, that he was furnishing her with means for a life-long burial in the glooms of the cloister. The poet gazed upon her for a moment quite bewildered, and then said, with one of those beaming smiles which irradiated his pale, intellectual face with rare beauty,

" I must recall my promise; I can not procure you admission into a religious community. You are not fitted for a nun. You can not understand the nature of the sacrifice which you are so eager to make. Will you become my wife ? My servants anger and neglect me. I am unable to enforce obedience. Were they under the control of a mistress, they would do their duty. My friends neglect me; I can not pursue them to reproach them for their abandonment. If they saw a pretty woman at the head of my household, they would make my home cheerful. I give you a week to decide."

Françoise returned to the convent bewildered, almost stunned. She was alone in the world, living upon reluctant charity. There was no one to whom she could confidingly look for advice. The future was all dark before her. Scarron, though crippled, was still young, witty, and distinguished as one of the most popular poets of the day. His saloon was the intellectual centre of the capital, where the most distinguished men were wont to meet. At the

close of the week Françoise returned an affirm-
ative answer. They were soon married. She
found apparently a happy home with her crippled but amiable husband. The brilliant circle in the midst of which she moved strength-
ened her intellect, enlarged her intelligence,
and added to that wonderful ease and gracefulness of manner with which she was by nature
endowed.

In the year 1660 Monsieur Scarron died.
He had lived expensively, and, as his income
was derived from a life annuity which ceased
at his death, his wife found herself again in
utter destitution. She was then forty-five years
of age. Madame de Montespan, who had frequently met her in those brilliant circles, which
had been rendered additionally attractive by
her personal loveliness and mental charms, persuaded the king to appoint Madame Scarron
governess for her children. A residence was
accordingly assigned her near the palace of the
Luxembourg, where she was installed in her
responsible office. She enjoyed a princely residence, horses, a carriage, and a suite of servants. The many attractions of Madame Scarron were not lost upon the king. He often
visited her, loved to converse with her, and

soon the jealousy of Madame de Montespan was intensely excited by the manifest fondness with which he was regarding the new favorite.

Greatly to the disgust of Madame de Montespan, whose influence was rapidly waning, the king appointed Madame Scarron to the responsible office of *Mistress of the Robes* to the dauphiness, Mary Ann of Bavaria, who was soon to arrive. He also conferred upon her the fine estate of Maintenon, with the title of Marchioness of Maintenon. It was now the turn of Madame de Montespan to experience the same neglect and humiliation through which she had seen, almost exultingly, the unhappy Madame de la Vallière pass.

The haughty favorite had reached her thirty-ninth year. The charms of youth were fast leaving her. Louis had attained his forty-second year. Bitter reproaches often rose between them. The king was weary of her exactions. He made several efforts, but in vain, to induce her to retire to one of the estates which he had conferred upon her. The daily increasing alienation led the king more frequently to seek the soothing society of the calm, gentle, serious Madame de Maintenon. Her fascinations of

MADAME DE MAINTENON.

1—18

person and mind won his admiration, while her virtues commanded his respect.

Such was the posture of affairs when preparations were made for the reception of the dauphiness with the utmost magnificence. The costumes of Madame de Maintenon were particularly remarked for their splendor, being covered with jewels and embroidered with gold.

"Madame de Maintenon, although in her forty-fifth year, had lost no charm save that of youth, which had been replaced by a stately grace, and a dignified self-possession that rendered it almost impossible to regret the lighter and less finished attractions of buoyancy and display. Her hands and arms were singularly beautiful; her eyes had lost nothing of their fire; her voice was harmoniously modulated, and there was in the whole of her demeanor unstudied ease, which was as far removed from presumption as from servility."*

Madame de Montespan was so annoyed by the honors conferred upon Madame de Maintenon that she was betrayed into saying, "I pity the young foreigner, who can not fail to be eclipsed in every way by her *Mistress of the Robes.*"

* Louis XIV. and the Court of France, vol. ii., p. 274.

Early in the year 1680 Madame de Maintenon and M. Bossuet, bishop of Meaux, who
had educated the dauphin, accompanied by a
suitable retinue, proceeded to Schelestadt to receive the dauphiness. Here the ceremony of
marriage by proxy was to be solemnized. The
king and the dauphin proceeded as far as Vit-
ry le Français to receive the bride. She was
not beautiful, "but she was," writes Madame
de Sévigné, "very graceful; her hands and
arms were exquisitely moulded. She had so
fine a figure, so admirable a carriage, such
handsome teeth, such magnificent hair, and so
much amiability of manner, that she was courteous without being insipid, familiar without
losing her dignity, and had so charming a deportment that she might be pardoned for not
pleasing at first sight."

Louis seemed quite delighted with his new
daughter-in-law, and devoted himself much to
her entertainment. She was accompanied by
her sister, the Princess of Tuscany, who was
extremely beautiful. The king, in conversation with Mary Ann, remarked, "You never
mentioned to me the fact that the Princess of
Tuscany was so singularly lovely." With tact
which gave evidence of her self-possession and

ready wit, the dauphiness replied, "How can I remember, sire, that my sister monopolized all the beauty of the family, when I, on my part, have monopolized all its happiness."

The young dauphiness had sufficient penetration soon to perceive that the attentions which the king was apparently devoting to her were due mainly to his desire to enjoy the society of the beautiful and agreeable *Mistress of the Robes*. The dauphiness was annoyed. Naturally of a retiring disposition, very fond of books and of music, she soon wearied of the perpetual whirl of fashion and frivolity, and gradually withdrew as much as possible from the society of the court. She imbibed a strong dislike to Madame de Maintenon, which dislike Madame de Montespan did every thing in her power to increase. The dauphiness became very unhappy. She soon found that her husband was a mere cipher, whom she could neither regard with respect nor affection. Louis XIV. allowed the dauphiness to pursue her own course. While ever treating her with the most punctilious politeness, he continued, much to her chagrin, and especially to that of Madame de Montespan, to manifest his admiration for Madame de Maintenon, and con-

stantly to seek her society. Thus the clouds
of discontent, jealousy, and bitter hostility shed
their gloom throughout the court. There was
splendor there, but no happiness.

It was a good trait in the character of the
king that he was affectionately attached to *all*
of his children. He provided for them sumptuously, and did every thing in his power to
provide abundantly for those of dishonorable
birth. Royal decrees pronounced them legitimate, and they were honored and courted as
princes of the blood.

Mademoiselle de Blois, a daughter of Madame de la Vallière, was one of the most beautiful and highly accomplished women ever
seen at the French court. Her mother had
transmitted to her all her many virtues and
none of her frailties. Tall and slender, her
figure was the perfection of grace. A slightly pensive air enhanced the charms of a countenance remarkably lovely, and of a bearing in
which were combined the highest attractions
of self-respect and courtly breeding. Her
voice was music. Her hands and feet were
finely modeled. Several foreign princes had
solicited her hand. But the king, her father,
had invariably declined these offers. He de-

clared that the presence of his daughter was essential to his happiness—that he could not be separated from her.

In 1680 Mademoiselle de Blois was married to the Prince de Conti, nephew of the great Condé. It was as brilliant a marriage as exalted rank, gorgeous dresses, superb diamonds, and courtly etiquette could create. The king could not have honored the nuptials more had he been giving a daughter of the queen to the proudest monarch in Europe. Her princely dowry was the same as would have been conferred on such an occasion. It amounted to five hundred thousand golden crowns. This was the same sum which the Spanish monarchy assigned Maria Theresa upon her marriage with the King of France.

It is difficult to imagine what must have been the emotions of Madame de la Vallière when she heard, in her narrow cell, the details of the brilliant nuptials of her child. Her loving heart must have experienced conflicting sensations of joy and of anguish. Madame de la Vallière had also a son, Count Vermandois. He became exceedingly dissipated, so much so as to excite the severe displeasure of the king. Rumor says that on one occasion he had the

audacity to strike the dauphin. The council
condemned him to death. Louis XIV., through
paternal affection, commuted the punishment
to imprisonment for life. The report was
spread that he had died of a contagious disease, while he was privately conveyed to the
prison of St. Marguerite, and subsequently to
the Bastile, his face being ever concealed under an iron mask. Here he died, it is said, on
the 19th of November, 1703, after an imprisonment of between thirty and forty years. The
true explanation of this great historical mystery will probably now never be ascertained.

The story of the "Man with the Iron Mask"
is one of the most remarkable in the annals of
the past. Probably no information will ever
be obtained upon this subject more full than
that which Voltaire has given. He says that
a prisoner was sent in great secrecy to the chateau in the island of St. Marguerite; that he
was young, tall, and of remarkably graceful
figure. His face was concealed by an iron
mask, with coils of steel so arranged that he
could eat without its removal. Orders were
given to kill him instantly if he should announce who he was. He remained at the chateau many years in close imprisonment.

In 1690, M. St. Mars, governor of the prison at St. Marguerite, was transferred to the charge of the Bastile in Paris. The prisoner, ever masked, was taken with him, and was treated on the journey with the highest respect. A well-furnished chamber was provided for him in that immense chateau. The governor himself brought him his food, and stood respectfully like a servile attendant while he ate. The captive was extremely fond of fine linen and lace, and was very attentive to his personal appearance. Upon his death the walls of his chamber were rubbed down and whitewashed. Even the tiles of the floor were removed, lest he might have concealed a note beneath them.

It is very remarkable that, while it can not be doubted that the prisoner was a person of some great importance, no such personage disappeared from Europe at that time. It is a plausible supposition that the king, unwilling to consign his own son to death, sent him to life-long imprisonment; and that the report of his death by a contagious disease was circulated that the mother might be saved the anguish of knowing the dreadful fate of her child. Still there are many difficulties connected with this explanation, and there is

none other which has ever satisfied public curiosity.

Madame de Montespan had eight children,
who were placed under the care of Madame
de Maintenon. Her eldest son, Count de Vix-
en, died in his eleventh year. Her second son,
the Duke de Maine, was a lad of remarkable
character and attainments. He loved Madame
de Maintenon. He did not love his mother.
Unfeelingly he reproached her with his ignoble birth. Madame de Montespan, though still
a fine-looking woman, brilliant, witty, and always conspicuous for the splendor of her equipage and her attire, felt every hour embittered
by the consciousness that her power over the
king had passed away. She regarded the serious, thoughtful Madame de Maintenon as her
successful rival, though her social relations with
the king were entirely above reproach.

The character of the discarded favorite is developed by the measure she adopted to lure the
susceptible and unprincipled monarch from the
very agreeable society of Madame de Maintenon. In the department of Provence there
was a young lady but eighteen years of age,
Mary Angelica Roussille. She was of such
wonderful beauty that its fame had reached

Paris. Her parents had educated her with the one sole object of rendering her as fascinating as possible. They wished to secure for her the position of a maid of honor to the queen, hoping that by so doing she would attract the favor of the king. Madame de Montespan heard of her. She plotted to bring this young and extraordinary beauty to the court, that, by her personal charms, she might outrival the mental and social attractions of Madame de Maintenon. She described her intended protegé to the king in such enthusiastic strains that his curiosity was roused. She was brought to court. The monarch, satiated by indulgence, oppressed by ennui, ever seeking some new excitement, was at once won by the charms of the beautiful Mary Angelica. She became an acknowledged favorite. He lavished upon her gifts of jewels and of gold, and dignified her with the title of the *Duchesse de Fontanges*. The court blazed again with splendor to greet the new favorite; and, let it not be forgotten, to meet this royal splendor, millions of peasants were consigned to hovels, and life-long penury and want.

There was a constant succession of theatric shows, ballets, and concerts. Mary Angelica

was a gay, frivolous, conceited, heartless girl,
who recklessly squandered the gold so profusely poured into her lap. The insolent favorite
even ventured to treat the queen with disdain,
assuming the priority. In the streets she made
a truly regal display in a gorgeous carriage
drawn by eight cream-colored horses, while the
clustering ringlets, the floating plumes, and the
truly radiant beauty of the *parvenue* duchess
attracted all eyes. If she had ever heard, she
refused to heed the warning voice of the proph-
et, saying, "Know thou that for all these things
God will bring thee into judgment."

The scheme of Madame de Montespan had
succeeded far more fully than she had expected or desired. The absorption of the king in
the new-comer was so entire that the discarded
favorite was tortured with new pangs of jealousy and remorse. Implacably she hated the
Duchess of Fontanges. With her sharp tongue
she mercilessly cut the luxurious beauty, who
had intelligence enough to feel the sarcasms
keenly, but had no ability to retort. A disgraceful quarrel ensued, in which the most vul-
gar epithets and the grossest witticisms were
bandied between them. The king himself at
length found it necessary to interpose. He ap-

plied to Madame de Maintenon for counsel and aid. She had quietly attended to her duties, observing all that was passing, but taking no part in these shameful intrigues. Conscious that any attempt to influence Madame de Montespan, hardened as she was in her career, would be futile, she ventured to address herself to the young and inexperienced Duchess de Fontanges. Gently she endeavored to lead her to some conception of the enormity of the life she was leading, and of the indecency of compromising the king and the court by undignified brawls.

The vain and heartless beauty received her counsels with bitter derision and passionate insult, and attributed every annoyance to which, as she averred, she was continually subjected, to the jealous envy of those with whose ambitious views she had interfered ; more than hinting that Madame de Maintenon herself was among the number. She was, however, only answered by a placid smile, and instructed to remember that those who sought to share her triumphs and her splendor must be content at the same time to partake her sin. It was a price too heavy to pay even for the smiles of a monarch. In vain did the flushed and furious beauty plead the example of others, higher born and more noble than herself. The calm and unmoved monitress instantly availed herself of this hollow argument to bid her, in her turn, to set an example which the noblest and the best-born might be proud to follow.

"And how can I do this?" was the sullen inquiry.

"By renouncing the society of the king," firmly replied Madame de Maintenon. "Either you love him, or you love him not. If you love him, you should make an effort to save both his honor and your own. If you do not love him, it will cost you no effort to withdraw from the court. In either case you will act wisely and nobly."

"Would not any one believe who heard you," passionately exclaimed the duchess, "that it was as easy to leave a king as to throw off a glove?"*

This was the only reply. The mission of Madame de Maintenon had entirely failed. The proud, unblushing beauty, whose effrontery passed all bounds, was greatly enraged against Madame de Maintenon; and when she

* Louis XIV. and the Court of France.

perceived that the king was again beginning to take refuge in her virtuous society and conversation, she vowed the most signal vengeance.

But the day of retribution soon came—far sooner than could have been expected. The guilty and pampered duchess was taken ill—hopelessly so, with a sickness that destroyed all her beauty. She became sallow, pallid, gaunt, emaciate, haggard. The selfish, heartless king wished to see her no more. He did not conceal his repugnance, and quite forsook her. The humiliation, distress, and abandonment of the guilty duchess was more than she could bear. She begged permission, either sincerely or insincerely, to retire to the convent of Port Royal. Louis, whose crime was far greater than that of his wrecked and ruined victim, was glad to be rid of her. But she was too far gone, in her rapid illness, to be removed. It was soon manifest that her life was drawing near to its close. She begged to see the king once more before she died.

Louis XIV. dreaded every thing which could remind him of that tomb toward which all are hastening, and especially did he recoil from every death-bed scene. The wretched man would not have listened to the plea of the dy-

ing girl had not the remonstrances of his confessor constrained him. Thus, reluctantly, he
entered the dying chamber. He found Mary
Angelica faded, withered, and ghastly—all
unlike the radiant beauty whom for a few
brief months he had almost worshiped. Ego-
tist as he was, he could not restrain his tears.
Her glassy eyes were riveted upon his countenance. Her clammy hand almost convulsively clasped his own. Her livid lips quivered in
their last effort as she besought him to pay
her debts, and sometimes to remember her.
Louis promised all she asked. As she sank
back upon her pillow, she gasped out the declaration that she should die happy, as she saw
that the king could weep for her. Immediately after she fell into a swoon and died.

The exultation of Madame de Montespan
at her death was so indecent and undisguised
as to excite the disgust of the king. Her very
name became hateful to him. Wicked man
as he was, Louis XIV. believed in Christianity,
and in its revelations of responsibility at the
bar of God. He was shocked, and experienced
much remorse in view of this death-bed without repentance. He could not conceal from
himself that he was in no inconsiderable de

gree responsible for the guilt which burdened the soul of the departed. His aversion to Madame de Montespan was increased by the report, then generally circulated, that the duchess had died from poison, administered through her agency. The poor victim of sin and shame was soon forgotten in the grave. The court whirled on in its usual round of frivolous and guilty pleasures, such as Babylon could scarcely have rivaled.

The supremacy of Madame de Maintenon over Louis XIV. was that of a strong mind over a feeble one. The king had many very weak points in his character. He was utterly selfish, and the slave of his vices. Madame de Maintenon, with much address, strove to recall him to a better life. In these efforts she was much aided by the king's confessor, Père la Chaise. This truly good man reminded the king that he had already passed the fortieth year of his age, that his youth had gone forever, that he would soon enter upon the evening of his days, and that, as yet, he had done nothing to secure his eternal salvation. He had already received many warnings as he had followed one after another to the grave. The king was naturally thoughtful, and perhaps

1—19

even religiously inclined. Not a few events
had already occurred calculated to harrow his
soul with remorse. He had seen his mother
die, one of the saddest of deaths. He had
seen his sister Henrietta, his brother's bride,
whom he had loved with more than a brother's
love, writhing in death's agonies, the victim of
poison. He had followed several of his children to the grave. Madame de la Vallière,
whom he had loved as ardently as he was capable of loving any one, now a ruined, heart-
broken victim of his selfishness and sin, was
consigned to living burial in the glooms of the
cloister. He could not banish from his mind
the dreadful scenes of the death of the Duchess of Fontanges.

Just at this time the dauphiness gave birth
to a son. This advent of an heir to the throne
caused universal rejoicing throughout the court
and the nation. It is melancholy to reflect
that the people, crushed and impoverished as
they were by the most atrocious despotism,
were so unintelligent that they regarded their
oppressors with something of the idolatrous
homage with which the heathen bow before
their hideous gods.

The king himself, at times, manifested a kind

of tender interest in the people, who were so
mercilessly robbed to maintain the splendor
of his court and the grandeur of his armies
Upon the birth of the young prince, who received the title of the Duke of Burgoyne, the
populace of Paris crowded to Versailles with
their rude congratulations. Every avenue was
thronged with the immense multitude. They
even flooded the palace and poured into the
saloons. The king, whose heart was softened
by the birth of a grandson to whom the crown
might be transmitted, received all very graciously.

The birth of an heir to the crown added
much to the personal importance of the dauphiness. But, neglected by her husband and
annoyed by the scenes transpiring around her,
she was a very unhappy woman. No efforts
on the part of the court could draw her from
the silence and gloom of her retirement. Madame de Maintenon and the king's confessor,
Père la Chaise, were co-operating in the endeavor to lure the king from his life of guilty
indulgence into the paths of virtue. Fortunately, at this time the monarch was attacked
by severe and painful illness. Death was to
him truly the king of terrors. He was easily

influenced to withdraw from his criminal relations with one whom he had for some time
been regarding with repugnance. Madame de
Maintenon was deputed to inform Madame de
Montespan of the king's determination never
again to regard her in any other light than that
of a friend.

It was a very painful and embarrassing commission for Madame de Maintenon to fulfill.
But the will of the king was law. She dis-
charged the duty with great delicacy and kind-
ness. Deeply mortified as was the discarded favorite, she was not entirely unprepared for the
announcement. She had for some time been
painfully aware of her waning influence, and
had been preparing for herself a retreat where
she could still enjoy opulence, rank, and power.

In pursuit of this object, she had determined
to erect and endow a convent. The sisterhood,
appointed by her and entirely dependent upon
her liberality, would treat her with the deference due to a queen. The king had lavished
such enormous sums upon her that she had
large wealth at her disposal. She had already
selected a spot for the convent in the Faubourg
St. Germain, and had commenced rearing the
edifice. It so happened that the corner-stone

was laid at the very moment in which the unhappy Duchess de Fontanges was breathing
her last. Madame de Montespan had no idea
of taking the veil herself. The glooms of the
cloister had for her no attractions. Her only
object was to rear a miniature kingdom, where
she, having lost the potent charms of youth and
beauty, could still enjoy an undisputed reign.

The marchioness already owned a dwelling,
luxuriously furnished, which the king had presented her, in the Rue St. Andre des Arcs.
Her wealth was so great that, in addition to
the convent, she also planned erecting for herself a magnificent hotel, in imitation of the palace of the Tuileries. The estimated expense
was equal to the sum of one million five hundred thousand dollars at the present day.

The workmen upon the convent were urged
to the most energetic labor, and the building
was soon completed. The marchioness gave
it the name of St. Joseph. One room was
sumptuously furnished for her private accommodation. She appointed the abbess. The
great bell of the convent was to ring twenty
minutes whenever she visited the sisterhood.
As the founder of the community, she was to
receive the honors of the incense at high mass

and vespers.   The marchioness richly enjoyed this adulation, and was a frequent visitor at the convent.

The king, having recovered from his illness, decided upon a journey to Flanders.   Oppressed with ennui, he sought amusement for himself and his court.   He wished also to impress his neighbors by an exhibition of his splendor and power.   The queen, with the dauphin and dauphiness, attended by their several suites, accompanied him on this expedition.   Madame de Montespan was excessively chagrined in finding her name omitted in the list of those who were to make up the party.   But the name of Madame de Maintenon headed the list of the attendants of the princess.

The gorgeous procession, charioted in the highest appliances of regal splendor, swept along through cities and villages, every where received with triumphal arches, the ringing of bells, the explosions of artillery, and the blaze of illuminations till the sea-port of Dunkirk was reached.   Here there was a sham-fight between two frigates.   It was a serene and lovely day.   The members of the royal suite, from the deck of a bark sumptuously prepared for their accommodation, witnessed with much

delight the novel spectacle. At the close, the
king repaired to one of the men-of-war, upon
whose deck a lofty throne was erected, draped
with a costly awning. Here the splendor-loving monarch, surrounded by that ceremonial
and pageantry which were so dear to him, received the congratulations of the dignitaries of
his own and other lands upon his recent recov-
ery from illness. At the end of a month the
party returned to Versailles.

Devoted as Louis XIV. was to his own selfish gratification, he was fully aware of the de-
pendence of that gratification upon the aggrandizement of the realm, which he regarded as
his private property. Upon this tour of pleasure he invested the city of Luxembourg with
an army of thirty thousand men, and took it
after a siege of eight days. He then overrun
the Electorate of Treves, demolished all its
fine fortifications, and by the energies of pil-
lage, fire, and ruin, rendered it impossible for
the territory hereafter to render any opposition
to his arms. The destructive genius of Louvois had suggested that these unnecessary spo-
liations would tend to increase the authority
of his royal master by inspiring a greater terror of his power.

Sickness and death of the queen, Maria Theresa.

Soon after this, the queen, Maria Theresa, was suddenly taken sick. Her indisposition, at first slight, rapidly increased in severity, and an abscess developed itself under her arm. The pain became excruciating. Her physician opened a vein and administered an emetic at 11 o'clock in the morning. It was a fatal prescription. At 3 o'clock in the afternoon she died. As this unhappy queen, so gentle, so loving, so forgiving, was sinking away in death, she still, with woman's deathless love, cherished tenderly in her heart the memory of the king. Just as she was breathing her last, she drew from her finger a superb ring, which she presented to Madame de Maintenon saying,

"Adieu, my very dear marchioness. To you I confide the happiness of the king."

Maria Theresa was one of the most lovely of women. Her conduct was ever irreproachable. Amiable, unselfish, warm-hearted, from the time of her marriage she devoted herself to the promotion of the happiness of her husband. His neglect and unfaithfulness caused her, in secret, to shed many tears. Naturally diffident, and rendered timid by his undisguised indifference, she trembled whenever the king approached her. A casual smile from him filled her with delight. The king could not be insensible to her many virtues. Perhaps remorse was mingled with the emotions which compelled him to weep bitterly over her death. As he gazed upon her lifeless remains, he exclaimed,

"Kind and forbearing friend, this is the first sorrow that you have caused me throughout twenty years."

The royal corpse lay in state at Versailles for ten days. During this time perpetual masses were performed for the soul of the departed from 7 o'clock in the morning until dark. The king had reared the gorgeous pal-

PALACE OF VERSAILLES.

ace of Versailles that he might not be annoyed, in his Babylonian revelry, by the sight of
the towers of St. Denis. But God did not allow the guilty monarch to forget that kings as
well as peasants were doomed to die. The
king was compelled to accompany the remains
of Maria Theresa from the sumptuous palace,
where she had found so splendid and so unhappy a home, to the gloomy vaults of the abbey, where, in darkness and silence, those remains were to moulder to dust.

The queen was forgotten even before she
was buried. The gay courtiers, anxious to
banish as speedily as possible from their minds
all thoughts of death and judgment, sought, in
songs, and mirth, and wine, to bury even the
grave in oblivion. The funeral car was decorated with the most imposing emblems of
mourning. A numerous train of carriages
followed, filled with the great officers of the
crown and with the ladies of the royal household. The procession was escorted by a brilliant and numerous body of mounted troops.

" But nothing could exceed the indecency
with which the journey was performed. From
all the carriages issued the sounds of heartless
jest and still more heartless laughter. The

troops had no sooner reached the plain of St. Denis than they dispersed in every direction, some galloping right and left, and others firing at the birds that were flying over their heads."*

The king, on the day of the funeral, in the insane endeavor to obliterate from his mind thoughts of death and burial, ordered out the hounds and plunged into the excitement of the chase. His horse pitched the monarch over his head into a ditch of stagnant water, dislocating one of his shoulders.

About this time, Jean Baptiste Colbert, the king's minister of finance, and probably the most extraordinary man of the age, died, worn out with toil, anxiety, and grief. Few men have ever passed through this world leaving behind them such solid results of their labors. As minister of finance, he furnished the king with all the money he needed for his expensive wars and luxurious indulgence. As superintendent of buildings, arts, and manufactures, he enlarged the Tuileries, completed the gorgeous palace of Versailles, reared the magnificent edifices of the Invalides, Vincennes, and Marly, and founded the Gobelins. These and many other works of a similar nature he per-

* Memoirs of Mademoiselle de Montpensier.

formed, though constantly struggling against the jealousy and intrigues of powerful opponents.

The king seldom, if ever, manifested any gratitude to those who served him. Colbert, in the 64th year of his age, exhausted by incessant labor, and harassed by innumerable annoyances, was on a dying bed. Sad reflections seemed to overwhelm him. Not a gleam of joy lighted up his fading eye. The heavy taxes he had imposed upon the people rendered him unpopular. He could not be insensible to imprecations which threatened to break up his funeral and to drag his remains ignominiously through the streets. The king condescended, as his only act of courtesy, to send a messenger to ask tidings of the condition of his minister. As the messenger approached the bed, the dying sufferer turned away his face, saying,

"I will not hear that man spoken of again. If I had done for God what I have done for him, I should have been saved ten times over. Now I know not what may be my fate."

The day after his death, without any marks of honor, his remains were conveyed, in an ordinary hearse, to the church of St. Eustache. A few of the police alone followed the coffin.

Genoa had offended the king by selling powder to the Algerines, and some ships to Spain. Louis seized, by secret warrant, *lettre de cachet,* the Genoese embassador, and plunged him into one of the dungeons of the Bastile. He then sent a fleet of over fifty vessels of war to chastise, with terrible severity, those who had offended him. The ships sailed from Toulon on the 6th of May, 1684, and entered the harbor of Genoa on the 19th. Immediately there was opened upon the city a terrific fire. In a few hours fourteen thousand bombs were hurled into its dwellings and its streets. A large portion of those marble edifices, which had given the city the name of *Genoa the Superb,* were crumbled to powder. Fourteen thousand soldiers were then disembarked. They advanced through the suburbs, burning the buildings before them. The whole city was threatened with total destruction. The authorities, in terror, sent to the conqueror imploring his clemency. The haughty King of France demanded that the Doge of Genoa, with four of his principal ministers, should repair to the palace of Versailles and humbly implore his pardon. The doge, utterly powerless, was compelled to submit to the humiliating terms.

Chapter IX.

The Revocation of the Edict of Nantes.

IT is the undisputed testimony of all the con-
temporaries of Madame de Maintenon that
she possessed a character of rare excellence.
Her personal attractions, sound judgment, instinctive delicacy of perception, and conversational brilliance, gave her a certain supremacy wherever she appeared.   The fidelity with
which she fulfilled her duties, her high religious principles, and the bold, yet tender remonstrances with which she endeavored to reclaim
the king from his unworthy life, excited first
his astonishment, and then his profound admiration.

Every day the king, at three o'clock, proceeded to the apartments of Madame de Maintenon,
and, taking a seat in an arm-chair, sat in a reclining posture, sometimes silently watching
the progress of her tapestry-work, and again
engaged in quiet conversation.   Occasionally
some of Racine's tragedies were read.   The

king took a listless pleasure in drawing out Madame de Maintenon to remark upon the merits or defects of the production.

"In truth, a weariness of existence was rapidly growing upon Louis XIV. He had outlived his loves, his griefs, and almost his ambition. All he wanted was repose. And this he found in the society of an accomplished, judicious, and unassuming woman, who, although he occasionally transacted business in her presence with Louvois, never presumed to proffer an opinion save when he appealed to her judgment, and even then tendered it with reluctance and reserve."*

Upon the death of the queen the dauphiness was raised to the first rank at court. Still she was gloomy and reserved. No allurements could draw her from her retirement. Madame de Maintenon was a very decided Roman Catholic, and was very much influenced by the king's confessor, Père la Chaise, who seems to have been a man of integrity and of conscientiousness, though fanatically devoted to what he deemed to be the interests of the Church. In former reigns the Protestants had endured

* Louis XIV. and the Court of France, by Miss Pardoe, vol. ii., p. 339.

from the Catholics the most dreadful persecu-
tions. After scenes of woe, the recital of which
causes the blood to curdle in one's veins, Henry IV., the grandfather of Louis XIV., feeling
the need of the support of the Protestants to
protect the kingdom from the perils by which
it was surrounded, and having himself been
educated a Protestant, granted the Protestants
the world-renowned Edict of Nantes.

By this edict, which took its name from the
place in which it was published, and which
was issued in April, 1598, certain privileges
were granted to the Protestants, which, in that
dark age, were regarded as extraordinarily lib-
eral.

Protestants were allowed liberty of conscience; that is, they were not to be punished
for their religious faith. In certain designated places they were permitted to hold public
worship. The highest lords of the Protestant
faith could celebrate divine service in their
castles. Nobles of the second rank could have
private worship provided but thirty persons
attended. Protestants were declared to be eli-
gible to offices of state, their children were to
be admitted to the public schools, their sick to
the hospitals, and their poor to the public char-

ities. In certain places they could publish books; they were allowed four academies for scientific and theological instruction, and were permitted to convoke synods for Church discipline.

The Catholic clergy were very indignant in view of these concessions. Pope Clement VIII. declared that the ordinance which permitted liberty of conscience to every one was the most execrable which was ever made.[*]

There were then seven hundred and sixty churches in France of the Protestant communion. No such church was allowed in Paris. Protestants from the city, rich and poor, were compelled to repair, for public worship, to the little village of Ablon, fifteen miles from the city. The Edict of Nantes probably cost Henry IV. his life. The assassin Ravaillac, who plunged his dagger twice into the bosom of the king, said, in his examination,

"I killed the king because, in making war upon the pope, he made war upon God, since the pope is God."

The Protestants were thrown into the utmost consternation by the death of Henry IV.

[*] History of the Protestants of France, by Professor G. de Félice, p. 275.

1—20

They apprehended the immediate repeal of
the edict, and a renewal of the massacre of St.
Bartholomew's Day. But the regent, Mary de
Medici, and the court immediately issued a decree confirming the ordinance. Louis XIII.
was then a child but eight and a half years
of age. As he came into power, he was urged
by the Jesuits to exterminate the Protestants.
But they were too powerful to be wantonly assailed. They held two hundred fortified places.
Many of the highest lords were among their
leaders. Their soldiers were renowned for val-
or, and their churches numbered four hundred
thousand men capable of bearing arms. It
was not deemed safe to rouse such a people to
the energies of despair. Still, during the reign
of Louis XIII., there were many bloody con-
flicts between the royal troops and the Protestants.

In this religious war, the Protestants, or Huguenots, as they were then called, defended
themselves so valiantly, that the king felt constrained, in October, 1622, to relinquish his attempt to subjugate the Protestants by force of
arms, and to confirm the Edict of Nantes.
The sword was scarcely sheathed ere it was
drawn again. All over France the Catholics

and Protestants faced each other upon fields of blood. The battle raged for seven years with every conceivable concomitant of cruelty and horror. The eyes of all Europe were directed to the siege of La Rochelle, in 1627, where the Huguenots made their most decisive stand. All that human nature could suffer was endured. When two thirds of the population of the city had perished, and the streets and dwellings were encumbered with the unburied dead, and the remaining soldiers, reduced to skeletons, could no longer lift their weapons, the city surrendered on the 28th of October, 1628.

By this war and the fall of La Rochelle, the Protestants were hopelessly weakened. Though they were deprived of many of their privileges, and were greatly diminished in numbers and influence, still the general provisions of the Edict of Nantes were not repealed.

In the year 1662, Louis XIV., then upon the throne, in recognition of some support which he had received from the Protestants, issued a decree in which he said,

"Inasmuch as our subjects of the pretended Reformed religion have given us proofs of

their affection and fidelity, be it known that,
for these reasons, they shall be supported and
guarded, as in fact we do support and guard
them, in the full enjoyment of the Edict of
Nantes."

The king had even appointed, the year before, two commissaries, the one a Catholic, the
other a Protestant, to visit every province, and
see that the requisitions of the Edict of Nantes
were faithfully observed. This seemed very
fair. But, in appointing these commissioners,
a Catholic was always appointed who was a
high dignitary of the state, a man of wealth
and rank, distinguished for his devotion to the
interests of the Catholic Church. On the other hand, the Protestant was always some poor
country gentleman, timid and irresolute, and
often one who had been secretly sold to the
court to betray his duties.

The Protestants had hoped much from the
influence of Madame de Maintenon over the
king, as she was the granddaughter of Agrip
pa d'Aubigné, one of the most illustrious de
fenders of the Calvinistic faith, and as she her
self had been a Protestant until she had at
tained the age of sixteen years.

But the king was fanatically Catholic, hoping, in some measure, to atone for his sins by his supreme devotion to the interests of the Church. Madame de Maintenon found it necessary, in promotion of her ambitious plans, to do all in her power to conceal her Protestant origin. She was fully aware of the king's great dislike to the Protestants, and of the necessity of cordially co-operating with him in these views. Still she could not refrain from manifesting some compassion at times for the sufferings of the friends of her earlier years.

Louis XIV., while assuring the Protestant powers of Europe that he would continue to respect the Edict of Nantes, commenced issuing a series of ordinances in direct opposition to that contract. First he excluded Protestants from all public offices whatever. A Protestant could not be employed as a physician, lawyer, apothecary, bookseller, printer, or even as a nurse. This decree was issued in 1680. In some portions of the kingdom the Protestants composed nearly the entire population. Here it was impossible to enforce the atrocious decree. In other places it led to riots and bloodshed.

This ordinance was followed by one forbid-ding marriages between Catholics and Protestants. Catholic servants were forbidden to serve in Protestant families, and Protestant servants could not be employed by Catholics.

Rapidly blow followed blow. On the 17th of June, 1680, the king issued the following ordinance: "We wish that our subjects of the pretended Reformed religion, both male and female, having attained the age of seven years, may, and it is hereby made lawful for them to embrace the Catholic Apostolic and Roman religion, and that to this effect they be allowed to abjure the pretended Reformed religion, without their fathers and mothers and other kinsmen being allowed to offer them the least hinderance, under any pretext whatever."

The effect of this law was terrible. Any malignant person, even a servant, could go into a court of justice and testify that a certain child had made the sign of the cross, or kissed an image of the Virgin, or had expressed a desire to enter the Catholic Church, and that child was immediately taken from its parents, shut up in a convent, and the parents were compelled to pay the expenses of its education. Even Madame de Maintenon availed herself of this law in wresting from her relative, the Marquis de Vilette, his children.

A decree was then issued that all Protestants who should become Catholics might defer the payment of their debts for three years, and for two years be exempt from taxation, and from the burden of having soldiers quartered upon them. To save the treasury from loss, a double burden of taxation and a double quartering of soldiers was imposed upon those Protestants who refused to abjure their faith.

If any Protestant was sick, officers were appointed whose duty it was to visit the sick-bed, and strive to convert the sufferer to the Catholic faith. Any physician who should neglect to give notice of such sickness was punished by a severe fine. The pastors were forbidden to make any allusions whatever in their sermons to these decrees of the court. Following this decree came the announcement that if any convert from Catholicism should be received into a Protestant Church, his property should be confiscated, he should be banished, and the privilege of public worship should no longer be enjoyed by that Church. Under this law several church edifices were utterly demolished.

One of the severest measures adopted against the Protestants was quartering brutal and fe-

rocious soldiers in their families. In March,
1681, Louvois wrote to the governor of Poitou
that he intended to send a regiment of cavalry
into that province.

"His majesty," he said, "has learned with
much satisfaction the great number of persons
who are becoming converts in your province.
He desires that you continue to give great care
to this matter. He thinks it best that the chief
part of the cavalry and officers should be lodged
in the houses of the Protestants. If, after a
just distribution, the Calvinists would have to
provide for ten soldiers, you can make them
take twenty."

The governor, Marillac, lodged from four to
ten dragoons in the house of every Protestant.
The soldiers were directed not to kill the people with whom they lodged, but to do every
thing in their power to constrain them to abjure Protestantism. Thus originated that system of *dragonnades* which has left an indeli-
ble stain upon the character of Louis XIV.,
and the recital of which has inspired every
reader with horror.

"The cavalry attached crosses to the muz-
zles of their muskets to force the Protestants
to kiss them. When any one resisted, they

thrust these crosses against the face and breasts of the unfortunate people. They spared children no more than persons advanced in years. Without compassion for their age, they fell upon them with blows, and beat them with the flat side of their swords and the butt of their muskets. They did this so cruelly that some were crippled for life."*

It does not reflect credit upon Madame de Maintenon that she was eager to enrich her friends from the spoils of these persecuted Christians. Her brother was to receive a present of one hundred and eight thousand francs ($21,600). This sum was then three or four times as much as the same amount of money now.

A law was now passed prohibiting the Protestants from leaving the kingdom, and condemning to perpetual imprisonment in the galleys all who should attempt to escape. France was ransacked to find every book written in support of Protestantism, that it might be burned. A representation having been made to the king of the sufferings of more than two millions of Protestant Frenchmen, he sternly replied,

* Histoire de l'Edit de Nantes, t. iv., p. 479.

" To bring back all my subjects to Catholic unity, I would readily, with one hand, cut off the other."

In some places the Protestants were goaded to an appeal to arms. With the most merciless butchery they were cut down, their houses razed, while some were put to death by lingering torture. In September, 1685, Louvois wrote,

" Sixty thousand conversions have taken place in the district of Bordeaux, and twenty thousand in that of Montauban. The rapidity with which they go on is such that, before the end of the month, there will not remain ten thousand Protestants in all the district of Bordeaux, where there were one hundred and fifty thousand the 15th of last month."

The Duke of Noailles wrote to Louvois, " The number of Protestants in the district of Nismes is about one hundred and forty thousand. I believe that at the end of the month there will be none left."

On the 18th of October, 1685, the king, acceding to the wishes of his confessor and other high dignitaries of the Church, signed the *Revocation of the Edict of Nantes*.

In the preamble to this fatal act, it was stated

Severe enactments against the Protestants.

"We see now, with the just acknowledgment we owe to God, that our measures have secured the end which we ourselves proposed, since the better and greater part of our subjects of the pretended Reformed religion have embraced the Catholic faith, and the maintenance of the Edict of Nantes remains therefore superfluous."

In this act of revocation it was declared that the exercise of the Protestant worship should nowhere be tolerated in the realm of France. All Protestant pastors were ordered to leave the kingdom within fifteen days, under pain of being sent to the galleys. Those Protestant ministers who would abjure their faith and return to Catholicism were promised a salary one third more than they had previously enjoyed. Parents were forbidden to instruct their children in the Protestant religion. Every child in the kingdom was to be baptized and educated by a Catholic priest. All Protestants who had left France were ordered to return within four months, under penalty of the confiscation of their possessions. Any Protestant layman, man or woman, who should attempt to emigrate, incurred the penalty of imprisonment for life.

This infamous ordinance caused an amount

of misery which can never be gauged, and inflicted upon the prosperity of France the most terrible blow it had ever received. Hundreds of thousands persevered in their faith, notwithstanding all the menaces of poverty, of the dungeon, and of utter temporal ruin. Only one year after the revocation, Marshal Vauban wrote,

"France has lost one hundred thousand inhabitants, sixty millions of coined money, nine thousand sailors, twelve thousand disciplined soldiers, six hundred officers, and her most flourishing manufactures."

From this hour the fortunes of Louis XIV. began manifestly to decline. The Protestant population of France at that time was between two and three millions. The edict of revocation was enforced with the utmost severity. Many noble-hearted Catholics sympathized with the Protestants in their dreadful sufferings, and aided them to escape. The tide of emigration flowed steadily from all the provinces. The arrival of the pastors and their flocks upon foreign soil created an indescribable sensation. From all the courts in Protestant Christendom a cry of indignation rose against such cruelty. Though royal guards were posted at the gates of the towns, on the bridges, at the fords of the rivers, and upon all the by-ways which led to the frontiers, and though many thousands were arrested, still many thousands escaped. Some heroic bands fought their way to the frontiers with drawn swords. Some obtained passports from kind-hearted Catholic governors. Some bribed their guards. Some traveled by night, from cavern to cavern, in the garb of merchants, pilgrims, venders of rosaries and chaplets, servants, mendicants.

Thousands perished of cold, hunger, and exhaustion. Thousands were shot by the soldiers. Thousands were seized and condemned to the dungeon or the galleys. The galleys of Marseilles were crowded with these victims of fanatical despotism. Among them were many of the most illustrious men in France, magistrates, nobles, scholars of the highest name and note.

The agitation and emigration were so immense that Louis XIV. became alarmed. Protestant England, Switzerland, Holland, Prussia, Denmark, Sweden, hospitably received the sufferers and contributed generously to the supply of their wants. "Charity," it is said, "draws from an exhaustless fountain. The more it gives the more it has to give."

It is now not possible to estimate the precise number who emigrated. Voltaire says that nearly fifty thousand families left the kingdom, and that they were followed by a great many others. One of the Protestant pastors, Antoine Court, placed the number as high as eight hundred thousand. A Catholic writer, inimical to the Protestants, after carefully consulting the records, states the emigration at two hundred and thirty thousand souls. Of these, 1580 were pastors, 2300 elders, and 15,000 nobles. It is also equally difficult to estimate the numbers who perished in the attempt to escape. M. de Sismondi thinks that as many died as emigrated. He places the number at between three and four hundred thousand.

As we have mentioned, the Protestants were compelled to place their children in Catholic schools, to be taught the Catechism by the priests. A new ordinance was soon issued, which required that the children, between five and sixteen, of all *suspected* of Protestantism, should be taken from their parents and placed in Catholic families. A general search was made throughout the kingdom for all books which could be deemed favorable to the Protestant faith. These were destroyed to the last copy. Thus perished many very valuable works. "The Bible itself, the Bible above all, was confiscated and burned with persevering animosity."[*]

But there is no power of persecution which can utterly crush out two or three millions of people. There were occasional reactions. Louis XIV. himself became, at times, appalled by the atrocities his dragoons were perpetrating, and he commanded more moderation. In some of the provinces where the Protestants had been greatly in the majority, the king found it very difficult to enforce his despotic and sanguinary code. The persecuted people who could not fly from the kingdom, some having given a compulsory and nominal assent to Catholicism, held secret assemblies in forests, on mountain summits, and in wild ravines. Some of the pastors ventured to return to France, and to assist in these scenes of perilous worship.

"On hearing this, the king, his ministers, and the Jesuits were transported with uncontrollable rage. Sentence of death was pro-

---

[*] Hist. of the Protestants of France, by Prof. G. De Félice.

nounced in the month of July, 1686, against
the pastors who had returned to France.
Those who lent them an asylum, or any assistance whatever, were condemned to the galleys
for life.   A reward of five thousand five hundred livres was promised to any one who seized
or secured the seizure of a minister.   The sentence of death was pronounced against all who
should be taken in any of these religious assemblies."*

Soldiers were sent in all directions to hunt
the Protestants.   " It was," writes Voltaire, " a
chase in a grand cover."   If the voice of prayer or of a psalm were heard in any wild retreat, the soldiers opened fire upon the assembly of men, women, and children, and hewed
them down without mercy with their blood-
stained swords.   In several of these encoun-
ters, three or four hundred men, women, and
young children were left dead and unburied
upon the spot.

If any sick persons, apparently near death,
refused to receive the sacraments of the Catholic Church from the hands of a Catholic
priest, should they recover, they were punished
with confiscation of property and consignment

* M. G. De Félice.

to the galleys for life. If they did not recover, their bodies were refused respectful burial, and were dragged on a hurdle and thrown into a ditch, to be devoured by carrion crows.

Many honorable Catholics cried out with horror against these enormities. All humane hearts revolted against such cruelty. The voice of indignant remonstrance rose from every Protestant nation. The French court became embarrassed. Two millions of people could not be put to death. The prisons were filled to suffocation. The galleys were crowded, and could receive no more. Many were transported to America.

The Jansenists remonstrated. The good Catholic bishops of Grenoble and St. Poins boldly addressed the curates of their dioceses, directing them not to force communion upon the Protestants, and forbidding all violence. Many pious curates refused to act the part of accusers, or to torment the dying with their importunities. But the Jesuits and the great mass of the clergy urged on the persecution.

Madame de Maintenon became greatly troubled by these atrocities, against which she did not dare to remonstrate. Louis XIV. was somewhat alarmed by the outcry which these

1—21

measures aroused from Protestant Europe, but
his pride revolted against making the admission, before his subjects and foreign courts,
that he could have been guilty of a mistake.
He could not endure the thought of humbling
himself by a retraction, thus confessing that
he had failed in an enterprise upon which he
had entered with such determination. Thus
influenced, the king, on the 13th of April, 1662,
issued a decree solemnly confirming the revocation of the Edict of Nantes. "Not one law
of torture and blood was abolished."

The king, meanwhile, urged by his growing
passion for Madame de Maintenon, determined
to remove from court Madame de Montespan,
whom he had come to thoroughly dislike. But
he had not the courage to announce his determination in person. He therefore commissioned Madame de Maintenon to make the painful
communication. She, shrinking from so unwelcome a task, persuaded the Marquis de Vivonne, brother of the marchioness, to break the
tidings to his sister. He invited her to take a
ride with him in his carriage, gradually introduced the subject, and at last plainly informed
her that she must either, of her own accord,
immediately and forever retire from Versailles,

or submit to the indignity of being arrested by
·the police and removed by them.

Madame de Montespan was in a fearful rage.
Though fully aware of her waning power over
the king, the menace of arrest and banishment
was an indignity the thought of which had
never entered her mind. But the calm firm-
ness of her brother soon convinced her of the
impotence of all exhibitions of indignation.
The splendor-loving marchioness was, as we
have mentioned already, wealthy. She was,
however, informed that the king had decided
to settle upon her an annual pension of six hundred thousand livres. When we consider the
comparative value of money then and now, it
is estimated that this amount was equivalent
to about four hundred and eighty thousand
dollars at the present day.

"Madame de Montespan," writes Miss Pardoe, " buried her face in her hands, and remained for a considerable time lost in thought.
When, at length, she looked up, her lips were
pale and her voice trembled. She had not shed
a tear, but her breast heaved, and she had evidently come to a decision. Folding her shawl
about her, she requested the marquis immediately to drive her to Versailles, it being neces-

sary, as she asserted, that she should collect her
money, her jewels, and her papers, after which
she declared that she was ready, for the sake
of her family, to follow his advice."

PARTERRE OF VERSAILLES.

They returned to the palace. Madame de
Maintenon hastened to her apartments. The
Marquis de Vivonne informed her of the success of his mission, and she communicated the
intelligence to the king.

The marchioness had been in her apartments
but about twenty minutes, when, to her surprise, the door opened, and the king entered
unannounced. The marchioness, with her own
graphic pen, has given an account of the sin-

Egotism and heartlessness of the king.

gular and characteristic interview which ensued.

The king came forward smiling very com-
placently at the thought that with so little embarrassment he was to get rid of a companion
whose presence had become an annoyance to
him—that he could discard her as easily as he
could lay aside a pair of soiled gloves. He
congratulated the marchioness upon the great
good sense she had shown in thus readily sun-
dering ties which, after existing for eighteen
years, had become embarrassing. He spoke of
their children as his property, and assured her
that he should do all in his power to promote
their welfare; that he had already, by act of
Parliament, conferred upon them statute legiti-
macy, and had thus effaced the dishonor of
their birth. He apologized for not having her
name mentioned in Parliament as their mother, this being impracticable, since she was the
wife of another man.

With smiling complacency, as if he were
communicating very gratifying intelligence, he
informed this crushed and discarded mother
that, since her children were now princes, they
would, of course, reside at court, and that she,
their dishonored mother, might occasionally be

permitted to visit them—that he would issue
an order to that effect. And, finally, he coolly
advised her to write to her husband, whom she
had abandoned eighteen years ago, soliciting a
renewal of their relationship, with the assurance that it was her intention to return to the
paths of virtue.

Almost gasping with indignation, the haughty marchioness succeeded in restraining herself
until the king had finished his harangue. She
then burst forth in a reply which astonished
and even alarmed the king.

"I am amazed," said she, "at the indifference with which a monarch, who boasts of his
magnanimity, can throw from him a woman
who has sacrificed every thing to his pleasure.
For two years your majesty, in devotion to
others, has been estranged from me, and yet
never have I publicly offered one word of ex-
postulation. Why is it, then, that I am now,
after silently submitting for two years to this
estrangement, to be ignominiously banished
from the court? Still, my position here has
become so hateful, through the perfidy and
treachery of those by whom I am compelled to
associate, that I will willingly consent never
again to approach the person of the king upon

condition that the odious woman who has supplanted me* shall also be exiled."

The proud monarch was enraged. Pale with anger, he replied, "The kings of Europe have never yet ventured to dictate laws in my palace, nor shall you, madame, subject me to yours. The lady whom I have too long suffered you to offend is as nobly born as yourself. If you were instrumental in opening the gates of the palace to her, you thus introduced there gentleness, talent, and virtue. This lady, whom you have upon every occasion slandered, has lost no opportunity to excuse and justify you. She will remain near the court which her fathers defended, and which her wise councils now strengthen. In seeking to remove you from the court, where your presence and pretensions have long since been misplaced, I wished to spare you the evidence of an *event* calculated to irritate your already exasperated nature. But stay you here, madame," he added, sarcastically, "stay you here, since you love great catastrophes and are amused by them. Day after to-morrow you will be more than ever a *supernumerary* in the palace."

* Madame de Maintenon.

This heartless announcement, that Madame de Maintenon was to take the place of Madame de Montespan in the affections of the king, and probably as his wedded wife, pierced, as with a dagger's point, the heart of the discarded favorite. She fell senseless to the floor. The king, without the slightest exhibition of sympathy, looked on impatiently, while her women, who were immediately summoned, endeavored to restore consciousness. As the unhappy marchioness revived, the first words which fell upon her ears were from the king, as he said,

"All this wearies me beyond endurance. She must leave the palace this very day."

In a frenzy of rage and despair, the marchioness seized a dessert-knife which chanced to lay upon the table, and, springing from the arms of her attendants, rushed upon her youngest child, the little Count de Toulouse, whom the king held by the hand, and from whom she was to be cruelly severed, and endeavored to plunge the knife into his bosom, exclaiming,

"Yes, I will leave this palace, but first—"

At that moment, before the sentence was finished, the door opened, and Madame de Maintenon, who had probably anticipated some tragic scene, sprang upon the wretched woman, seizing the knife with one hand, and with the other thrusting the child away. The maniacal marchioness was seized by her attendants. The king tottered to the chimney-piece, buried his face in his hands, and, from a complicity of emotions not easily disentangled, wept convulsively.

Madame de Maintenon's hand was cut by the knife. As she was binding up the bleeding wound with her handkerchief, the half-delirious marchioness said to her, referring to the fact that the king had at first been unwilling to receive her as the guardian of the children,

"Ah! madame, had I believed what the king told me fourteen years ago, my life would not have been in your power to-day."

Madame de Maintenon, her eyes suffused with tears, looked sadly upon her, then taking her hand, pressed it feelingly, and, without uttering a word, left the apartment. The king followed her. The heart-broken marchioness, in most imploring tones, entreated the king not thus to leave her. He paid no heed to her supplications. The agitation of this scene threw Madame de Montespan into such a burning fever that for several days she could not be removed from her bed of pain and woe.

CHAPTER X.

THE SECRET MARRIAGE.

THE king exerted all his powers of persuasion to induce Madame de Maintenon to
enter into the same relations with him which
Madame de Montespan had occupied. At last
she declared, in reply to some passionate reproaches on his part, that she should be under
the necessity of withdrawing from the court
and retiring to the cloister, rather than continue to expose herself to a temptation which
was destroying her peace of mind and undermining her health. Under these circumstances
the king had been led to think of a private
marriage. At first his pride revolted from the
thought. But in no other way could he secure
Madame de Maintenon.

Rumors of the approaching marriage were
circulated through the court. The dauphin
expostulated with his father most earnestly
against it, and succeeded in inducing the king
to consult the Abbé Fenelon and Louvois.
They both protested against the measure as

compromising the dignity of the monarch and the interests of the nation. Bossuet, however, urged the marriage. Boldly he warned the king against entering again into such connections as those which had hitherto sullied his life, wounded his reputation, and endangered his eternal welfare.

Pure as Madame de Maintenon was, the devotion of the king to her was so marked that her reputation began to suffer. She felt the unjust imputations cast upon her very keenly. The king at last resolved that it should be so no longer. Having come to a decision, he acted very promptly. It was a cold night in January, 1686. A smothering snow-storm swept the streets of Paris. At half past ten o'clock a court messenger entered the archiepiscopal palace with a sealed packet, requesting the archbishop to repair immediately to Versailles to perform the marriage ceremony. The great clock of the Cathedral was tolling the hour of eleven as the prelate entered his carriage in the darkness and the storm. At half past twelve he reached the gate of the chateau. Here Bontems, the first valet de chambre of the king, conducted the archbishop to the private closet of his majesty. Madame de Maintenon was there in full dress. Louis XIV. stood by her side. In the same apartment were the Marquis de Montechevreuil and the king's confessor, Père la Chaise.

Miss Pardoe thus describes the scene that ensued :

"As the eye of the king rested upon the archbishop, he exclaimed, 'Let us go.' Taking the hand of the lady, he led her forward through the long suite of rooms, followed by the other actors in this extraordinary scene, who moved on in profound silence, thrown for an instant into broad light by the torch carried by Bontems, and then suddenly lost in the deep darkness beyond its influence. Nothing was to be heard as the bridal party proceeded save the muffled sound of their footsteps, deadened by the costly carpets over which they trod. But it was remarked that as the light flashed for an instant across the portraits of his family which clothed the walls, Louis XIV. glanced eagerly and somewhat nervously upon them, as though he dreaded the rebuke of some stern eye or haughty lip for the weakness of which he was about to become guilty."

The marriage ceremony was performed by the Archbishop of Paris. There were eight persons present as witnesses, most of them of high distinction. The king was in the forty-eighth year of his age, and Madame de Maintenon in her fifty-second. The marriage was celebrated with all the established ceremonies of the Church, the solemnization of the mass, the exchange of marriage rings, and the pronouncing of the benediction by the archbishop. A magnificent suite of apartments was prepared for Madame de Maintenon at Versailles. She retained her own liveries, but thenceforward appeared in public only in the carriage of the king. Though by her own private attendants she was addressed as " your majesty," she was never publicly recognized as the queen. The king addressed her simply as *Madame*.

Though the morning after the nuptials the astounding rumor spread through the court that the king had actually married the *Widow Scarron*, still there were no positive vouchers found for the fact. As she was never recognized as the queen, for a long time many doubts rested upon the reality of the marriage.

It was a matter of necessity that Madame de Montespan should call upon Madame de Maintenon, and pay her respects to her as the real though unrecognized wife of the monarch.

Dressed in her richest robes, and glittering with
jewels, the discarded favorite entered the apartment of her hated rival. The king was seated
by her side. His majesty rose, bowed formal-
ly, and took his seat. Madame de Maintenon
did not rise, but, with a slight flush upon her
cheek, motioned to Madame de Montespan to
take a seat upon a *tabouret* which stood near
by. The king scarcely noticed her. Madame
de Maintenon addressed her in a few words of
condescension. The unhappy visitor, after a
short struggle to regain her composure, rose
from the humble stool upon which she had
been seated, and, repeating the stately rever-
ences which etiquette required, withdrew from
the room.

With crushed heart she retired to her apartment, and, weeping bitterly, threw herself upon
a sofa. She soon sent for her son, the Duke
du Maine, hoping to hear, from his lips at least,
words of sympathy. But the duke, who had
reproached his mother with his dishonorable
birth, and who, by a royal decree, had been recognized as a prince, was not at all disposed to
cultivate intimate relations with that mother,
now that the memory of disgrace only would
be perpetuated by that recognition. Without

the exhibition of the slightest emotion, the duke addressed his mother in a few cold, formal words, and left her. The marchioness summoned her carriage, and left Versailles and the court forever. As she cast a last look upon the palace, she saw the king standing at the balcony of a window watching her departure.

The reader will be interested in learning the routine of a day as passed by this most sumptuous of earthly kings amidst the splendors of Versailles. At eight o'clock in the morning the under valets carefully entered the bedchamber, opened the shutters, replenished the wood fire, if cold, and removed the ample refreshments which were always placed by the royal bedside in case the king should need food during the night.

The first valet then entered, carefully dressed, and took his stand respectfully by the side of the bed-curtains. At half past eight precisely he drew the curtains and awoke the king, assuming always that he was asleep. The valet then immediately retired to an adjoining room, where several distinguished members of the court were in waiting, and communicated to them the important intelligence that the king no longer slept.

The folding doors were thrown open, and
the dauphin, attended by his two sons, the eldest of whom was entitled *Monsieur*, and the
youngest the Duke of Chartres, entered, and
inquired of the king how he had passed the
night. They were immediately followed by
the Duke du Maine and the Count de Toulouse, sons of Madame de Montespan, and by
the first lord of the bedchamber and the grand
master of the robes. They were succeeded by
the first valet of the wardrobe, and by several
officers, each bearing a portion of the royal
vestments. The two medical attendants of the
king, the physician and surgeon, also entered
at the same time.

The king, still remaining pillowed in his gorgeous bed, held out his hands, and his first valet de chambre poured upon them a few drops
of spirits of wine, holding beneath them a basin
of silver. The first lord of the bedchamber
presented a vase of holy water, with which the
king made the sign of the cross upon his brow
and breast. His majesty then repeated a short
prayer. A collection of wigs was presented to
him. He selected the one which he wished to
wear. As the king rose from his couch, the
first lord of the bedchamber drew upon him

his dressing-gown, which was always a richly embroidered and costly robe.

The king then sat down, and, holding out one sacred foot after the other, his valet, Bontems, drew on his stockings and his slippers of embroidered velvet. The monarch condescended to place upon his head, with his own hand, the wig which he had selected. Again the devout monarch crossed himself with holy water, and, emerging from the balustrade which inclosed the bed, seated himself in a large arm-chair. He was now prepared for what was called *The First Entrée*.

The chief lord of the bedchamber, with a loud voice, announced *The First Entrée*. A number of courtiers, who were peculiarly favored, were then admitted to the distinguished honor of seeing his majesty washed and shaved. The barber of the king removed his beard and gently washed his face with a sponge saturated with spirits of wine and water. The king himself wiped his face with a soft towel, while Bontems held the glass before him.

And now the master of the robes approached to dress the king. Those who had been present at what was called the *petit lever* retired. A new set of dignitaries, of higher

1—22

name and note, crowded the anteroom to enjoy the signal honor of being present at the
Grand Entrée, that is, of witnessing the sublime ceremony of seeing shirt, trowsers, and
frock placed upon his sacred majesty.

Three of the highest officers of the court
stood at the door, attended by several valets and
door-keepers of the cabinet.   Admission to the
Grand Entrée was considered so great an honor
that even princes sought it, and often in vain.

As each individual presented himself, his
name was whispered to the first lord of the
bedchamber, who repeated it to the king.
When the monarch made no reply the visitor
was admitted, and the duke walked back to
his station near the fireplace, where he marshaled the new-comers to their several places
in order to prevent their pressing too closely
about his majesty.   Princes and governors,
marshals and peers, were alike subjected to
this tedious and somewhat humiliating ceremony, from which three individuals alone were
excepted, Racine, Boileau, and Mansard.   On
their arrival at the guarded door they simply
scratched against the panel, when the usher
threw open the folding door, and they stood in
the presence of the monarch.

RACINE.

BOILEAU.

In the mean time, a valet of the wardrobe delivered to a gentleman of the chamber the socks and garters, which the *gentleman* presented to the monarch, and which socks his majesty deigned to draw on himself. Even with his own hand he clasped the garters with their diamond buckles. Etiquette did not allow the king to unclasp them at night. The head valet de chambre enjoyed the privilege of unclasping the garter of the right leg, while a more humble attendant performed the same office for the left leg.

A distinguished officer of the household presented the monarch with his *haut de chausses* (breeches), to which silk stockings were attached; the king drew them on; another gentleman put on his shoes; another gentleman buckled them. Two pages, richly dressed in crimson velvet embroidered with gold, removed the slippers which the king had laid aside.

And now came the royal breakfast. Two officers of the household entered, in picturesque attire, one bearing a loaf of bread on an enameled salver, and another a folded napkin between two enameled plates. The royal cupbearer handed a golden vase, richly decorated, to one of the lords. He poured into it a small

quantity of wine and water. Another lord
tasted of it, to prove that it contained no poison. The vase was then carefully rinsed, and
being again filled with the wine and water,
was presented to the king on a gold salver.

His majesty drank. Then the dauphin, who
was always present at these solemnities, handed his hat and gloves to the first lord in waiting, and presented the monarch with a napkin
with which to wipe his lips. Breakfast was a
very frugal repast. Having partaken of these
slight refreshments, the king laid aside his
dressing-gown. One of his lordly attendants
then assisted him in removing his night-shirt
by the left sleeve. It was Bontems's peculiar
privilege to draw it off by the right sleeve.

The royal shirt, which had been carefully
warmed, was then given to the first lord. He
presented it to the dauphin, who approached
and presented it to the king. Some one of the
higher lords, previously designated for the
honor, assisted the king in the arrangement of
his shirt and breeches. A duke enjoyed the
honor of putting on his inner waistcoat. Two
valets presented the king with his sword, vest,
and blue ribbon. A nobleman then stepped
forward and buckled on the sword, assisted in

putting on the vest, and placed over his shoulders a scarf bearing the cross of the Holy Ghost in diamonds, and the cross of St. Louis.

The king then drew on his under coat, with the assistance of the grand master of the robes, adjusted his cravat of rich lace, which was folded round his neck by a favorite courtier, and finally emptied into the pockets of the loose outer coat, which was presented to him for that purpose, the contents of those which he had worn the previous day. He then received two handkerchiefs of costly point from another attendant, by whom they were carried on an enameled saucer of oval shape called salve. His toilet once completed, Louis XIV. returned to the *ruelle* of his bed, where he knelt down upon two cushions already prepared for him, and said his prayers; all the bishops and cardinals entering within the balustrade in his suite, and reciting their devotional exercises in a suppressed voice.

The king, being thus dressed, retired from his chamber to his cabinet. He was followed, in solemn procession, by all those dignitaries of Church and State who had enjoyed the privilege of the *Grand Entrée*. He then issued the orders of the day, after which all withdrew

excepting some of his children, whom a royal
decree had legitimatized and raised to the rank
of princes, with their former tutors or governors.

In the mean time a crowd of courtiers were
assembled in the great gallery of Versailles,
to accompany the king to mass. The captain
of the royal guard awaited orders at the door
of the cabinet. At 12 o'clock the door was
thrown open, and the king, followed by a
splendid retinue, proceeded to the chapel.

The service was short. At one o'clock the
king returned to his room, and dined sumptuously and alone. He was waited upon, at the
table, by the first gentleman of the chamber.
Sometimes the dauphin or other lords of highest rank were present, but they stood respectfully at a distance. No one was permitted to
be seated in the royal presence. The brother
of the king stood at times by the chair of his
majesty, holding his napkin for him. Upon
the king's twice requesting him to be seated,
he was permitted to take a seat upon a stool,
behind the king, still holding his napkin.

Upon rising from the table the king repaired to the grand saloon, where he tarried for a
few moments, that persons of high distinction,

who enjoyed the privilege of addressing him, might have an opportunity to do so. He then returned to his cabinet. The door was closed, and the king had a brief interview with his children, of whom he was very fond. He then repaired to the kennel of his dogs, of whom he was also fond, and amused himself, for a time, in feeding them and playing with them.

He now made some slight change in his dress. A small number of persons, of high rank, enjoyed the distinguished honor of being present in his chamber as the monarch, with all suitable stateliness of ceremony, exchanged one royal garment for another. The carriage awaited the king in the marble court. He descended by a private staircase. His craving for fresh air was such that he took a drive whatever the weather. Scarcely any degree of heat or cold, or floods of rain, could prevent him from his drive, or his stag-hunt, or his overlooking the workmen. Sometimes the ladies of his court rode out with him on picnic excursions to the forests of Fontainebleau or Marly.

Upon returning from the drive, the king again changed his dress and repaired to his cabinet. He then proceeded to the apartments of Madame de Maintenon, where he remained

conversing with her, or reading, and sometimes
transacting business with his minister, until ten
o'clock. The hour for supper had now arrived.
The house-steward, with his badge of office in
hand, gave the information to the captain of
the guard. He, entering the royal presence
from the antechamber, announced the fact to
the king, and opened wide the door. After the
delay of a quarter of an hour, which etiquette
required, his majesty advanced to the supper-
room. During the quarter of an hour which
had elapsed, the officers of the household had
made preparations for the royal repast by tast-
ing the bread and the salt, and by testing the
plates, the fork, the spoon, the knife, and the
tooth-pick of the king, so as to be assured that
no poison could be thus conveyed.

As the king, preceded by the house-steward
and two ushers with flambeaux, entered the
supper-room, he found there awaiting him the
princes and princesses of France, with a numerous assemblage of courtiers, gentlemen, and
ladies. The king, having taken his seat, requested the others to be seated also. Six no-
blemen immediately stationed themselves at
each end of the table, to wait upon the king.
Each one, as he presented a dish to the king,

first tasted of it himself. When the king wished for a drink, his cup-bearer exclaimed aloud, "Drink for the king." Two of the principal officers, making a profound obeisance, approached his majesty, one bearing an enameled cup and two decanters upon a salver. The other poured out the wine, tasted it, and presented the goblet to the king. With another low salutation, the two officers replaced the decanters upon the sideboard.

The repast being finished, the king rose, and, preceded by two guards and an usher, and followed by all the company, proceeded to the bed-chamber. He there bowed adieu to the company, and, entering the cabinet, took a seat in a large arm-chair. The members of the royal family were introduced. His brother, Monsieur, was permitted to take an arm-chair. All the rest remained standing except the princesses, who were indulged with stools. After an hour or so of such converse as these stately forms would admit, the king, about midnight, went again to feed his dogs. He then retired to his chamber, with great pomp said his prayers, and was undressed and put to bed with ceremonies similar to those with which he had been dressed in the morning.

Such was the ordinary routine of the life of the king at Versailles. Its dreary monotony was broken by occasional fêtes, balls, and theatric shows. Madame de Maintenon testifies to the almost insupportable tedium of such a life. "If you could only," she exclaims, "form an idea of what it is!"

Magnificent apartments were prepared for Madame de Maintenon at Versailles, opposite the suite of rooms occupied by the king. Similar arrangements were made for her in all the royal palaces. Royalty alone could occupy arm-chairs in the presence of the sovereign. In each of her apartments there were two such, one for the king and the other for herself. The king often transacted business with his minister, Louvois, in her room. She had sufficient tact never to express an opinion, or to take a part in the conversation except when appealed to.

Madame de Maintenon was exceedingly anxious that the king should publicly recognize her as his wife. It is said that the king, tormented by the embarrassments which the secret marriage had brought upon him, seriously contemplated this. His minister, Louvois, remonstrated even passionately against such a

recognition. At the close of a painful interview upon this subject, he threw himself upon
his knees before his majesty, and, presenting to
him the hilt of a small sword which the minister usually wore, exclaimed,

"Take my life, sire, that I may not become
the witness of a disgrace which will dishonor
your majesty in the eyes of all Europe."

Others of the most influential members of
the court joined in the opposition, and so stren-
uously that the king commanded Madame de
Maintenon never again to allude to the subject.

Premature old age was fast advancing upon
the king, though he had as yet attained only
his forty-ninth year. He was tortured by the
gout. He was also attacked by a very painful
and dangerous internal malady. His sufferings were dreadful. It became necessary for
him to submit to a perilous surgical operation.
The king met the crisis with much heroism.
Four persons only, including Madame de Maintenon, were present during the operation. Indeed, the greatest precautions had been adopted to keep the fact that an operation was to be
performed a profound secret. During the operation the king uttered not a groan. It was
successful. In gratitude he conferred upon

the skillful operator who had relieved him from anguish and saved his life an estate valued at more than fifty thousand crowns.

Weary of every thing else, the king now sought to find some little interest in building. The renowned architect, Mansard, whose genius still embellishes our most beautiful edifices, was commissioned to erect a pavilion on the grounds of Versailles in imitation of an Italian villa. Thus rose, within a year, the *Grand Trianon*, which subsequently became so celebrated as the favorite rural residence of Maria Antoinette.

Most men who, with vast wealth, attempt to build a mansion which shall eclipse that of all their neighbors, and which shall be perfect in all the appliances of comfort and luxury, find themselves, in the end, bitterly disappointed. This was pre-eminently the case with Louis XIV. The palace of Versailles, still unfinished, had already cost him countless millions. But it did not please the king. It had cold and cheerless grandeur, but no attractions as a home. The king looked with weary eyes upon the mountain pile of marble which had risen at his bidding, and found it about as uncongenial for a home as would be the Cathedral of

THE TRIANON.

MARLY.

Nôtre Dame. Disgusted with the etiquette
which enslaved him, satiated with sensual indulgence, and having exhausted all the foun-
tains of worldly pleasure, with waning powers
of body and of mind, it is not possible that any
thing could have satisfied the world-weary king.

He had other palaces. None suited him.
The Tuileries and the Louvre were in the heart
of the noisy city. The banqueting hall at St.
Germain overlooked the sepulchre of St. Denis, where the grave-worm held its banquet.
Fontainebleau was at too great a distance from
the capital. To reach it required a carriage
drive of four or five hours. Vincennes, notwithstanding the grandeur of the antique,
time-worn castle, was gloomy in its surround-
ings, inconvenient in its internal arrangements
—a prison rather than a palace.

About nine miles from Paris, upon the left
bank of the Seine, there reposed the silent village of Marly. The king selected that as the
spot upon which he would rear a snug "hermitage" to which he could retire "from noise
and tumult far." The passion for building is
a fearful passion, which often involves its victim in ruin. The plans of the king expanded
under his eye. The little hermitage became a

spacious palace, where a court could be entertained with all the appliances of regal elegance.

But dark and stormy days were rapidly
gathering around the path of the king. He
became involved in war with Germany. The
complicated reasons can scarcely be unraveled.
The king sent his son, the dauphin, at the head
of one hundred thousand men, to invade Holland. Situated upon both sides of the Rhine
there was a territory called the Palatinate. It
embraced one thousand five hundred and nine-
ty square miles, being not quite so large as the
State of Delaware. It contained an intelligent, industrious, and prosperous population of
a little over three hundred thousand. The
beautiful city of Manheim was the capital of
the province.

Though the dauphin was nominally at the
head of the invading army, that the glory of
its victories might redound to his name, the
ablest of the French generals were associated
with him, and they, in reality, took the direction of affairs. One city after another speedily fell into the hands of the French. The king
mercilessly resolved, and without any justifica-
tion whatever, to convert the whole province
into a desert. An order was issued by the

king that every city, village, castle, and hut
should be laid in ashes.

It was midwinter—the month of February,
1689. There were many beautiful cities in
the province, such as Manheim, Philipsbourg,
Franckendal, Spire, Treves, Worms, and Op-
pendeim. There were more than fifty feudal
castles in the territory, the ancestral homes of
noble families. The citizens had but short
warning. Houses, furniture, food, all were
consumed. The flames rose to heaven, calling
upon God for vengeance. Smouldering ruins
every where met the eye. Men, women, and
children wandered starving through the fields.

Nearly all Europe soon became banded
against this haughty monarch, and he found it
necessary to raise an army of four hundred
thousand men to meet the exigencies.

Intoxicated by the pride of past success, he
thought that he should be able to force upon
England a Roman Catholic king, and the Roman Catholic faith, and thus expel *heresy* from
England, as he dreamed that he had expelled
it from France. He equipped a fleet, and
manned it with twenty thousand soldiers, to
force upon the British people King James II.,
whom they had indignantly discarded.

358   L o u i s XIV.   [1689.

Civil war in France.   Complications of the royal family.

Civil war was now also desolating unhappy
France. The Protestants, bereft of their children, robbed of their property, driven from
their homes, dragged to the galleys, plunged
into dungeons, broken upon the wheel, hanged
upon scaffolds, rose in several places in the
most desperate insurrectionary bands. And
the man who was thus crushing beneath the
heel of his armies the quivering hearts of the
Palatinate, and who was drenching his own
realms with tears and blood, was clothed in
purple, and faring sumptuously, and reclining
upon the silken sofas of Marly and Versailles.
It is not strange that Faith, with uplifted hands
and gushing eyes, should have exclaimed, "O
Lord, how long!"

The singular complication of the royal family, with the various mothers and the various
children, some of which children were recognized by royal decree as princes, and some of
whom were not, filled the palaces with bickerings, envyings, and discontent in every form.
The unhappy dauphiness, who had long been
immersed in the profoundest gloom, at last
found a welcome retreat in the grave. Neither her husband nor the king shed a single
tear over her remains, which were hurried to
the vaults of St. Denis.

Chapter XI.

Intrigues and Wars.

THE treasury of the king was empty. Extravagant building, a voluptuous court, and all the enormous expenses of civil and foreign wars, had quite exhausted the finances of the realm. It became necessary to call upon the cities for contributions. New offices were invented, which were imposed upon the wealthy citizens, and for which they were compelled to pay large sums. Even the massive silver plate and furniture, which had attracted the admiration of all visitors to Versailles, were sent to the Mint and coined. Most of the value of these articles of ornament consisted of the skill with which the materials had been wrought into forms of beauty. In melting them down, all this was sacrificed, and nothing remained but the mere value of the metal. Large as were the sums attained by these means, they were but trifling compared with the necessities of the state.

Louvois, the minister of Louis, had for a long

time held the reins of government. It was
through his influence that the king had been
instigated to revoke the Edict of Nantes, to
order the dragonnades, and to authorize those
atrocities of persecution which must ever expose the name of Louis XIV. to the execrations of humanity. It was Louvois who, from
merely contemptible caprice, plunged France
into war with Germany. It was through his
persuasions that the king was induced to order
the utter devastation of the Palatinate.

But the influence of Louvois was now on the
wane. The jealous king became weary of his
increasingly haughty assumptions. The con-
flagration of the Palatinate raised a cry of indignation which the king could not but hear.
The city of Treves had escaped the flames.
Louvois solicited an order to burn it. The
king refused to give his consent. Louvois insolently gave the order himself. He then informed the king that he had done so that he
might spare the conscience of the king the pain
of issuing such an edict.

Louis was furious. In his rage he forgot all
the restraints of etiquette. He seized from the
fireplace the tongs, and would have broken the
head of the minister had not Madame de Main-

LOUIS XIV. DIRECTING THE SIEGE.

tenon rushed between them. The king ordered
a messenger immediately to be dispatched to
countermand the order. He declared that if
a single house were burned, the head of the
minister should be the forfeit. The city was
saved.

In 1691 the French army was besieging
Mons. The king visited the works. The haughty minister, unintimidated even by the menace
of the tongs, ventured to countermand an order which the king had issued. The lowering
brow of the monarch convinced him that his
ministerial reign was soon to close.

The health of the minister began rapidly to
fail. He became emaciate, languid, and deeply depressed. A few subsequent interviews
with the king satisfied him that his disgrace
and ruin were decided upon. Indeed, the king
had already drawn up the *lettre de cachet*
which was to consign him to the Bastile.
About the middle of June, 1691, Louvois met
the king in his council chamber, and, though
the monarch was unusually complaisant, Louvois so thoroughly understood him that he retired to his residence in utter despair. Scarcely had he entered his apartment ere he dropped
dead upon the floor. Whether his death were

caused by apoplexy, or by poison administered
by his own hand or that of others, can never
be known. The king forbade all investigation
of the case.

Immediately after the death of Louvois, the
king began to devote himself to business with
an energy which he had never before manifested. Madame de Maintenon made some
farther efforts to induce him to proclaim their
marriage, but she soon perceived that nothing
would induce him to change his resolution, and
she accepted the situation. Louis now yielded
more than ever to her influence; but he was
always apprehensive that she might be engaged
in some secret intrigue, and kept a vigilant
watch over her. In letters to a friend, she gives
some account of her splendid misery.

"The king is perpetually on guard over me.
I see no one. He never leaves my room. I
am compelled to rise at five in the morning in
order to write to you. I experience more than
ever that there is no compensation for the loss
of liberty."

Again she writes, in reference to the weary
routine of court life: "The princesses who
have not attended the hunt will come in, followed by their cabal, and wait the return of

the king in my apartment in order to go. to dinner. The hunters will come in a crowd, and will relate the whole history of their day's sport, without sparing us a single detail. They will then go to dinner. Madame de Dangeau will challenge me, with a yawn, to a game of backgammon. Such is the way in which people live at court."

It will be remembered that the king and queen had an only son, the dauphin. He was a man of ignoble character and of feeble mind. Still, as heir to the throne, he was, next to the king, the most important personage in the realm. The dauphin had three sons, who were in the direct line of succession to the crown. These were Louis, duke of Burgoyne, Philip, duke of Anjou, and Charles, duke of Berri.

The eldest, the Duke of Burgoyne, who, of course, next to the dauphin, was heir to the throne, was thirteen years of age. The king selected for his wife Adelaide, the daughter of the Duke of Savoy, a remarkably graceful, beautiful, and intelligent child of eleven years. The pretty little girl was brought to France to spend a few months in the court previous to her marriage, which was to take place as soon as she should attain her twelfth year. She came in great splendor, with her retinue, her court, and her ladies of honor. Both the king and Madame de Maintenon were charmed with the princess. Sumptuous apartments were assigned her in the palace of Versailles. Madame de Maintenon wrote to the Duchess of Savoy,

"The king is enchanted with her. He expatiates on her deportment, her grace, her courtesy, her reserve, and her modesty. She has all the graces of girlhood, with the perfections of a more mature age. Her temper appears as perfect as her figure promises one day to become. She only requires to speak to display the extent of her intellect. I can not resist thanking your royal highness for giving us a child who, according to all appearance, will be the delight of the court, and the glory of the century."

The king resolved that the festivities at the marriage of these two children should be the most splendid which France had ever witnessed. He announced the intention of appearing himself, upon the occasion, in the most sumptuous apparel which the taste and art of the times could furnish. This intimation was sufficient for the courtiers. Preparations were

made for such a display of folly and extravagance as even alarmed the king. All ordinary
richness of dress, of satin, and velvet, and embroidery of gold, was discarded for fabrics of
unprecedented costliness, for bouquets of diamonds, and wreaths of the most precious gems.

"I can not understand," exclaimed the king,
"how husbands are mad enough to suffer
themselves to be ruined by the folly of their
wives."

The marriage took place between the bride
of twelve years and the bridegroom of fourteen at six o'clock in the evening of the 7th of
December, 1697. The ceremony was performed in the chapel of the palace at Versailles.
The ensuing festivals exceeded in magnificence
all that Versailles had previously witnessed.
But there was no rejoicing among the people.
They listened, some silently, some sullenly,
some murmuringly, to the chiming bells and
the booming cannon. The elements of discontent and wrath were slowly beginning to collect for bursting forth one hundred years later,
in that most sublime of moral tempests, the
French Revolution.

The grand avenue to Versailles day after
day was crowded with gorgeous equipages.

At night it blazed with illuminations. The highest ingenuity was taxed to devise new scenes of splendor and amusement, which followed each other in rapid succession. Three days after the marriage, the king gave a special assembly which was to eclipse all the rest. All the ladies were directed to appear in dresses of black velvet, that the precious gems, which were almost literally to cover those dresses, might sparkle more brilliantly. The great gallery of Versailles was illuminated by four thousand wax-lights. The young bride wore upon her apron alone jewels estimated at a sum equal to fifty thousand dollars.

On the 1st of November, 1700, Charles II., the half crazed King of Spain, died, leaving no heir. The pope, Innocent XII., bribed by Louis XIV., sent a nuncio to the dying king, enjoining upon him to transmit his crown to the children of the Dauphin of France, as the legitimate heirs to the monarchy. As the Duke of Burgoyne was the direct heir to the throne of France, the second son of the dau phin, the Duke of Anjou, still a mere boy, was proclaimed King of Spain, with the title of Philip V.

On the 14th of the month the Spanish em-

bassador was summoned to an audience with
Louis XIV. at Versailles. The king presented his grandson to the minister, saying, " This,
sir, is the Duke of Anjou, whom you may salute as your king."

A large crowd of courtiers was soon assembled. The Spanish minister threw himself
upon his knees before the boy with expressions
of profound homage. There was a scene of
great excitement. The king, embracing with
his left arm the neck of the young prince,
pointed to him with his right hand, and said
to those present,

" Gentlemen, this is the King of Spain. His
birth calls him to the crown.* The late king
has recognized his right by his will. All the
nation desires his succession, and has entreated
it at my hands. It is the will of Heaven, to
which I conform with satisfaction."

The Duke of Anjou was quite delighted in

---

* The claim of the young prince was founded upon the fact
that his grandmother, Maria Theresa, was the eldest daughter of Philip IV. of Spain. She had, however, upon her marriage, renounced all claim to the succession. Her younger
sister, Margarita, had married the Emperor Leopold of Austria without this renunciation. The emperor claimed the
crown for her daughter, who had married the Elector of Bavaria. Hence the war of *The Spanish Succession.*

finding himself thus liberated from all the restraints of tutors and governors, and of being,
in his boyhood, elevated to the dignity of a
crowned king. As soon as these stately forms
of etiquette were concluded, and he was alone
with his brothers, he kicked up his heels and
snapped his fingers, exclaiming with delight,

"So I am King of Spain. You, Burgoyne,
will be King of France. And you, my poor
Berri, are the only one who must live and die
a subject."

The little prince replied, perhaps upon the
principle that "the grapes were sour," perhaps
because he had observed how little real happiness regal state had brought to his grandfather,

"That fact will not grieve me. I shall have
less trouble and more pleasure than either of
you. I shall enjoy the right of hunting both
in France and Spain, and can follow a wolf
from Paris to Madrid."

Preparations were immediately made for the
departure of the boy-king to take possession of
his Spanish throne and crown. The pomp-
loving French king had decided to invest the
occasion with great splendor. He regarded it
as a signal stroke of policy, and a great victory
on his part, that he had been enabled, notwith-

standing the remonstrances of other nations, to
place a French Bourbon prince upon the throne
of Spain, thus virtually uniting the two nations.
He thought he had thus extended the domain
of France to the Straits of Gibraltar. "Henceforth," exclaimed Louis XIV., exultingly,
"there are no more Pyrenees."

To his grandson, the new king, he said, "Be
a good Spaniard, but never forget that you
were born a Frenchman. Carefully maintain
the union of the two nations. Thus only can
you render them both happy."

There was a final meeting of the royal family to take leave of the young monarch as he
was departing for his realm. All the young
nobility of France, with a numerous military
escort, were to compose his brilliant retinue.
The Duchess du Maine, the legitimatized daughter of Madame de Montespan, and thus the half
brother of the dauphin, persuaded the dauphin
to invite her mother to the palace on this occasion. Here occurred the last interview between
the heartless king and his discarded favorite.

As the king made the tour of the room, he
found himself opposite Madame de Montespan.
She was greatly overcome by her emotions, and,
pale and trembling, was near fainting. The

king coldly and searchingly, for a moment,
fixed his eye upon her, and then said, calmly,

"Madame, I congratulate you. You are still
as handsome and attractive as ever. I hope
that you are also happy."

The marchioness replied, "At this moment,
sire, I am very happy, since I have the honor
of presenting my respectful homage to your
majesty."

The king, with his studied grace of courtesy,
kissed her hand, and continued his progress
around the circle. The monarch and his perhaps equally guilty victim never met again.
She lived twenty-two years after her expulsion
from the palace. They were twenty-two years
of joylessness. Her confessor, who seems to
have been a man of sincere piety, refused her
absolution until she had written to her husband, the Marquis de Montespan, whom she
had abandoned for the guilty love of the king,
affirming her heartfelt repentance, imploring
his forgiveness, and entreating him either to
receive her back, or to order her to any place
of residence which he should think proper.
The indignant marquis replied that he would
neither admit her to his house, nor prescribe
for her any future rules of conduct, nor suffer

her name ever again to be mentioned in his presence.

The reverend father compelled her, in atonement for her sins, to sit at a frugal table; to consecrate her vast wealth to objects of benevolence; to wear haircloth next her skin, and around her waist a girdle with sharp points, which lacerated her body at every movement. She was also daily employed in making garments of the coarsest materials with her own hands for the sick in the hospitals, and for the poor in their squalid homes.

The guilty marchioness was dreadfully afraid of death. Every night a careful guard of women watched her bedside. In a thunder-storm she would take an infant in her lap, that the child's innocence might be her protection. In the night of the 26th of May, 1707, she was attacked in her bed by very distressing suffocation. One of her sons, the Marquis of Antin, was immediately sent for. He found his mother insensible. Seizing a casket which contained her jewels, he demanded of an attendant the key. It was suspended around the neck of his dying mother, where she ever wore it. The young man went to the bedside, tore away the lace which veiled his mother's bosom, seized

the key, unlocked the casket, emptied its contents into his pockets, descended to his carriage,
and hurried away with the treasure, leaving his
mother to die without a relative to close her
eyes. An hour after she breathed her last.

The king was informed of the death of Madame de Montespan just as he was setting out
on a shooting excursion. "Ah! indeed," he
said, "and so the marchioness is dead. I
should have thought that she would have lasted longer. Are you ready, M. de la Roche-
foucald? I have no doubt that after this last
shower the scent will lie well for the dogs.
Come, let us be off at once."

We have slightly anticipated the chronolog-
ical sequence of events in this narrative of the
death of Madame de Montespan, which took
place in the year 1707. James II. of England
died in exile at St. Germain in September,
1701. The Prince of Orange then occupied
the British throne with the title of William
III. He formed what was called the "Grand
Alliance" against the encroachments of France.
For several years the war of the "Spanish
Succession" raged with almost unprecedented
fury throughout all Europe.

The king's health was now failing, and

FRONT VIEW OF ST. GERMAIN.

troubles in rapid succession came crowding upon him. His armies encountered terrible defeats. The king had thus far lived on friendly terms with his only brother Philip, duke of Orleans, the playmate of his childhood, and the submissive subject of maturer years. They were now both soured by misfortune. In a chance meeting at Marly they fell into a violent altercation respecting the conduct of one of the sons of the duke. It was their first quarrel since childhood. The duke was so excited by the event that he hastened to his palace at St. Cloud with flushed cheeks and trembling nerves, where he was stricken down by apoplexy. A courier was immediately dispatched to the king. He hastened to the bedside of his brother, and found him insensible.

Philip was two years younger than Louis. To see him die was a louder appeal to the conscience of the king than the view of St. Denis from the terrace at St. Germain. Death was, to this monarch, truly the king of terrors. He could not endure the spectacle of his brother's dying convulsions. Burying his face in his hands, he wept and sobbed bitterly. It was a midnight scene, or rather it was the sombre hour of three o'clock in the morning.

At 8 o'clock in the morning the king took his carriage and returned to Marly, and repaired immediately to the apartment of Madame de Maintenon. At 11 o'clock his physician arrived with the intelligence that the duke was dead. Again the king was overcome with emotion, and wept almost convulsively; but, soon recovering himself, he apparently resolved to make every effort to throw off these painful thoughts.

Notwithstanding the remonstrances of Madame de Maintenon, he persisted in his determination to dine, as usual, with the ladies of the court. Much to the astonishment of the ladies, he was heard, in his own room, singing an air from a recent opera which was far from funereal in its character.

In the month of May of this same year, 1701, the Duke of Anjou, the young King of Spain, who was uneasily seated upon his beleaguered throne, entered into a matrimonial alliance with Maria Louisa of Savoy, younger sister of Adelaide, the duchess of Burgoyne. She was of fairy-like stature, but singularly graceful and beautiful, with the finest complexion, and eyes of dazzling brilliance. Her mental endowments were also equal to her physical

charms. Louis XIV., ever anxious to retain
the control over the court of Spain, appointed
the Princess des Ursins to be the companion
and adviser of the young queen. This lady
was alike remarkable for her intelligence, her
sagacity, her tact, and her thorough acquaint-
ance with high and courtly breeding. The
young King of Spain was perfectly enamored
of his lovely bride. She held the entire control over him. The worldly-wise and experienced Princess des Ursins guided, in obedience
to the dictates of Louis XIV., almost every
thought and volition of the young queen.
Thus the monarch at Marly ruled the court at
Madrid.

While foreign war was introducing bank-
ruptcy to the treasury of France, civil war was
also desolating the kingdom. The sufferings
of the Protestants equaled any thing which had
been witnessed in the days of pagan persecution. The most ferocious of all these men, who
were breathing out threatenings and slaughter,
was the Abbé de Chayla. This wretch had
captured a party of Protestants, and, with them,
two young ladies from families of distinction.
They were all brutally thrust into a dungeon,
and were fettered in a way which caused ex-

treme anguish, and crushed some of their bones.
It was the 24th of July, 1702. At ten o'clock
in the evening, a party of about fifty resolute
Protestants, thoroughly armed, and chanting a
psalm, broke into the palace of the infamous ecclesiastic, released the prisoners from the dungeon vaults, seized the abbé, and, after compelling him to look upon the mangled bodies and
broken bones of his victims, put him to death
by a dagger-stroke from each one of his assail-
ants. The torch was then applied, and the palace laid in ashes.

Hence commenced the terrible civil war
called *The War of the Camisards*. The Protestants were poor, dispersed, without arms, and
without leaders. Despair nerved them. They
fled to rocks, to the swamps, the forests. In
their unutterable anguish they were led to fren-
zies of enthusiasm. They believed that God
chose their leaders, and inspired them to action.
Thus roused and impelled, they set at defiance
an army of twenty thousand men sent against
them.

The terrible war lasted two years. Fiends
could not have perpetrated greater cruelties
than were perpetrated by the troops of the
· king. It is one of the mysteries of divine prov-

idence that *one man* should have been permitted to create such wide-spread and unutterable
woe. Louis XIV. wished to exterminate Protestantism from his realms. Millions were made
wretched to an intensity which no pen can describe. Louis XIV. wished to place his grandson, without any legal title, upon the throne
of Spain. In consequence, Europe was deluged
in blood. Cities were sacked and burned.
Provinces were devastated. Hundreds of thousands perished in the blood of the battle-field.
The book of final judgment alone can tell how
many widows and orphans went weeping to
their graves.

The Pope Clement IX. fulminated a bull
against the Camisards, and promised the absolute remission of sins to those engaged in their
extermination. Protestant England and Holland sent words of cheer to their fellow-relig-
ionists. We can not enter into the details of
this conflict. The result was that the king
found it impossible to exterminate the Protestants, or to blot out their faith. A policy
of semi-tolerance was gradually introduced,
though in various parts of the kingdom the
persecuting spirit remained for several years
unbroken. The king, chagrined by the failure

of his plans, would not allow the word Protestant or Huguenot to be pronounced in his presence.

The distress in France was dreadful. A winter of unprecedented severity had even frozen
the impetuous waters of the Rhone. Provisions
commanded famine prices. The fields were
barren, the store-houses exhausted, the merchant ships were captured by the enemy, and
the army, humiliated by frequent defeats, was
perishing with hunger. The people became
desperate. The king was ignominiously lam-
pooned and placarded. He dared not appear
in public, for starving crowds gathered around
his carriage clamoring for bread. Even the
king and the nobility sent their plate to the
Mint. The exhaustion of the realm had become so complete that the haggard features of
want seemed to be staring in even at the windows of the palace. Madame de Maintenon
practiced so much self-denial as to eat only
oaten bread.

In April of 1711 the dauphin was taken sick
with apparently an attack of fever. It proved
to be malignant smallpox. After a brief sickness, which terrified and dispersed the court,
he died, almost alone, in a burning fever, with

a frightfully swollen face, and in delirium.
Even the king could not visit the dying chamber of his son. He fainted upon his sofa when
he heard that the dauphin was in his last agonies.

The terror-stricken courtiers fled from the
palace of Meudon, where the loathsome remains of the heir to the throne of France
awaited burial. The corpse was hurried into
a plain coffin, which was not even covered by
the royal pall. Not a single mourning coach
followed the only legitimate son of Louis XIV.
to the grave. He had two sisters, the Princess
of Conti and the Duchess of Bourbon Condé.
Neither of them ventured to join the funeral
procession of their only brother. He had three
sons, Louis, Philip, and Charles. Philip was
king of Spain. Louis and Charles were at
home. But they kept at a safe distance, as did
the king his father, from the meagre funeral
procession which bore, with indecent haste, the
remains of the prince to the vaults of St. Denis.

CHAPTER XII.

THE LAST DAYS OF LOUIS XIV.

UPON the death of the king's son, the Duke of Burgoyne assumed the title of Dauphin, which his father had previously borne, and became direct heir to the crown. He was a retiring, formal man, very much devoted to study, and somewhat pedantic. He was also religiously inclined. In his study, where he passed most of his time, he divided his hours between works of devotion and books of science. His sudden advent to the direct heirship to the French throne surrounded him with courtiers and flatterers. The palace at Meudon, where he generally resided, was now crowded with noble guests.

He became affable, frequently showed himself in public, entered into amusements, and was soon regarded as a general favorite. Taught by Madame de Maintenon, he succeeded, by his marked respect for the king and his submission to his slightest wishes, in gaining the good will of the homage-loving monarch. The years had rolled rapidly along, and the young dauphin was thirty years of age. He had three children, and, being irreproachable in his domestic relations, was developing a very noble character. The dauphiness had attain-- ed her twenty-seventh year. She was an ex tremely beautiful and fascinating woman.

The dauphiness was fond of snuff. On the 3d of February, 1712, the Duke de Noailles, a true friend, presented her with a box of Span- ish snuff, with which she was delighted. She left the box upon the table in her boudoir. It was there for a couple of days, she frequently indulging in the luxury of a pinch. On the 5th she was attacked with sudden sickness, ac- companied by shivering fits, burning fever, and intense pain in the head. The attack was so sudden and extraordinary that all the attend- ants thought of poison, though none ventured to give utterance to the surmise. For four days she grew worse, with frequent seasons of delirium. The dauphin was almost frantic. The king sat in anguish, hour after hour, at her bedside.

No remedies were of any avail. Her suffer- ings were so great that the dauphin could not remain in her dying chamber to witness her agony. She was greatly surprised when in-

formed that she must die. All the offices of
the Church were attended to. She received
the rite of extreme unction, and, in the wild-
ness of delirium, lost all recognition of those
who were around her. The king, bowed down
with anguish, was with difficulty prevailed
upon to retire. He had but reached the door
of the palace when she expired.

The king was now a world-weary, heart-
stricken old man, who had numbered more
than his threescore years and ten. He seemed crushed with grief, and his eyes were flooded with tears as he returned, with Madame de
Maintenon, to Marly. The apartment which
the dauphin paced in agony was immediately
above the dying chamber. As soon as the
death-struggle was over, he was induced to retire to Marly, that he might be spared the anguish of witnessing the preparations for the
funeral.

As the dauphin entered the chamber of the
king, the monarch was startled in witnessing
the change which had taken place in his appearance. His face was flushed with fever;
his eyes were dilated and inflamed, and livid
stains covered his face. It was manifest that
the same disease, whatever it was, which had

stricken down the dauphiness, had also attacked the dauphin. The malady made rapid
progress. In the intensity of his anguish, the
sufferer declared his entrails were on fire.
Conscious that his dying hour had come, he,
on the night of the 17th, partook of the sacrament of the Lord's Supper, and almost immediately expired.

The dreadful tidings were conveyed to the
king as he sat in the apartment of Madame de
Maintenon, with the younger brother of the
dauphin, Charles, the duke de Berri, by his
side. The king, anticipating the announcement, sat with his head bent down upon his
breast, and clasping almost convulsively the
hand of the prince who sat at his feet. Throwing his arms around the neck of the Duke de
Berri, the king exclaimed, in accents of despair,
" Alas ! my son, you alone are now left to me."

The Duke of Burgoyne had buried three
children. There were two then living. The
eldest, the Duke of Bretagne, was five years of
age. The youngest, the Duke of Anjou, had
just attained his second year. By the death
of the Duke of Burgoyne, his eldest child became the dauphin and the immediate heir to
the crown. The next day both of these chil-

dren were taken sick, evidently with the same
malady, whether of natural disease or the effect of poison, which had proved so fatal to
their parents. The eldest immediately died.
The same funeral car conveyed the remains of
the father, the mother, and the child to the
gloomy vaults of St. Denis.

The youngest child, the Duke of Anjou, by
the most careful nursing recovered to ascend
the throne with the title of Louis XV., and to
present to the world, in his character, one of
the most infamous kings who had ever worn
an earthly crown.

We have previously mentioned the death of
the king's only brother, Philip, duke of Orleans. He left a son, the Duke of Chartres.
Upon the death of the Duke of Orleans his
son inherited the title and the estate of his father. He was an exceedingly dissolute man.
Should all the legitimate descendants of the
king die, he would be heir to the throne.
With the exception of Philip, who was King
of Spain, and thus precluded from inheriting
the throne of France, all were now dead except the infant Duke of Anjou. The death
of that child would place the crown upon the
brow of Philip, duke of Orleans.

As it was evident that all these victims had died of poison, suspicion was so directed against the Duke of Orleans that the accusation was often hooted at him in the streets. There is, however, no convincing evidence that he was guilty. One of the daughters of the Duke of Orleans had married the Duke de Berri. She was as wicked as she was beautiful, and scarcely condescended to disguise her profligacy. The duke intercepted some letters which proved her guilty intimacy with an officer of her household. A violent quarrel took place in the royal presence. The husband kicked his wife with his heavy boot, and the king lifted his cane to strike the duke.

A sort of reconciliation was effected. The duchess, who, beyond all doubt, was a guilty woman, professed to be satisfied with the apologies which her husband made. Soon after they went on a wolf-hunt in the forest of Marly. Both appeared in high spirits. The run was long. Heated by the race and thirsty, the duke asked the duchess if she had any thing with her with which he could quench his thirst. She drew from the pocket of her carriage a small bottle, which contained, she said, an exquisite cordial with which she was always pro-

vided in case of over-fatigue. The duke drain-
ed it, and returned the empty bottle to the
duchess. As she took it she said, with a smile,
"I am very glad to have met you so oppor-
tunely."

Thus they parted. In a few hours the duke
was a corpse. It was so manifestly for the interest of the dissolute and unprincipled Duke
of Orleans that the princes which stood between him and the throne should be removed,
that all these cases of poisoning were attributed
to him. Indeed, one of the motives which
might have influenced his daughter, the Duchess de Berri, to poison her husband, whom she
loathed, may have been the hope of seeing her
father upon the throne. When the funeral
procession passed near the Palais Royal, the
residence of the duke, the tumult was so great
that it was feared that the palace might be
sacked.

The anguish of the duke, thus clamorously
assailed with the crime of the most atrocious
series of assassinations, was great. A friend,
the Marquis de Canillac, calling upon him one
day, found him prostrate upon the floor of his
apartment in utter despair. He knew that he
was suspected by his uncle the king, and by

the court as well as by the populace. At last
he went boldly to the king, and demanded that
he should be arrested, sent to the Bastile, and
put upon trial. The king sternly, and without
any manifestation of sympathy, refused, saying
that such a scandal should not, with his consent, be made any more public than it already
was. The king also recoiled from the idea of
having a prince of the blood royal tried for
murder.

As it was known that the king could not live
long, and a babe of but two years was to be his
successor—a feeble babe, who had already nar-
rowly escaped death by poison, the question of
the regency, during the minority of this babe,
and of heirship to the throne in case the babe
should die, became a matter of vast moment.
The court was filled with intrigues and plots.
The Duke of Orleans had his numerous parti-
sans, men of opulence and rank. He was but a
nephew of the king—son of the king's brother.

On the other hand was the Duke du Maine,
an acknowledged *son* of the king—the legiti-
mated son of Madame de Montpensier. But
no royal decree, no act of Parliament could
obliterate the stain of his birth. He had many
and powerful supporters, who, by his accession

to power, would be placed in all the offices of honor and emolument. Madame de Maintenon, in herself a host, was one of the most devoted of his friends. She had been his tutor. She had ever loved him ardently. He had also pledged her, in case of his success, that she should be recognized as Queen of France.

The monarch was harassed and bewildered by these contending factions. The populace took sides. The Duke of Orleans could not leave his palace without being exposed to the hootings of the rabble. He withdrew from his city residence, the Palais Royal, to the splendid palace of St. Cloud. He was accompanied by a magnificent train of nobles, and, being a man of almost boundless wealth, he established his court here in regal splendor.

There was no *proof* that the Duke of Orleans was implicated in the poisonings. The king was unwilling to receive evidence that his brother's son could be guilty of such a crime. Being superstitiously a religionist, the king recoiled from the attempt to place upon the throne a son of Madame de Montespan, who was the acknowledged wife of another man. He therefore favored the claims of the Duke of Orleans, and sent him word at St. Cloud that he recognized his innocence of the crime of which public rumor accused him.

It is, however, very evident that this was a measure of policy and not of sincere conviction. He entered into no friendly relations with the duke, and kept him at a respectful distance. The disastrous war of the Spanish Succession was now closed, through the curious complications of state policy. Philip VI. retained his throne, but France was exhausted and impoverished. The king often sat for hours, with his head leaning upon his hand, in a state of profound listlessness and melancholy. Famine was ravaging the land. A wail of woe came from millions whom his wars and extravagance had reduced to starvation.

The Duchess de Berri, the unblushing profligate, the undoubted murderess, was, as the daughter of the king's brother, the only legitimate princess left to preside over the royal court. She was fascinating in person and manners, with scarcely a redeeming virtue to atone for her undisguised vices.

" Thus the stately court of Anne of Austria, the punctilious circle of Maria Theresa, and the elegant society of the Duchess of Burgoyne were—at the very period of his life when Louis

XIV., at length disenchanted of the greatness and disgusted with the vices of the world, was seeking to purify his heart and to exalt his thoughts that they might become more meet for heaven—superseded by the orgies of a wanton, who, with unabashed brow and unshrinking eye, carried her intrigues into the very saloons of Marly."*

Madame de Maintenon resorted to every measure she could devise to induce the king to appoint her favorite pupil, the Duke du Maine, regent during the minority of the infant Duke of Anjou. The king was greatly harassed. Old, infirm, world-weary, heart-stricken, and pulled in opposite directions by powers so strong, he knew not what to do. At last he adopted a sort of compromise, which gave satisfaction to neither party.

The king appointed a council of regency, of which the Duke of Orleans was president. But the Duke du Maine was a member of the council, and was also intrusted with the guardianship and education of the young heir to the throne. This will was carefully concealed in a cavity opened in the wall of a tower of the state apartment. The iron door of this closet

* Louis XIV. and the Court of France, vol. ii., p. 588.

was protected by three keys, one of which was held by the president of the chambers, one by the attorney general, and one by the public registrar.

A royal edict forbade the closet to be opened until after the death of the king, and then only in the presence of the assembled Parliament, the princes, and the peers. The document had been extorted from the king. It was not in accordance with his wishes. Indeed, it satisfied no one. As he placed the papers in the hands of the president of the chambers, he said to him, gloomily,

"Here is my will. The experience of my predecessors has taught me that it may not be respected. But I have been tormented to frame it. I have been allowed neither peace nor rest until I complied. Take it away. Whatever may happen to it, I hope that I shall now be left in quiet."*

The advanced age of the king and his many infirmities rendered even a slight indisposition alarming. On the evening of the 3d of May, 1715, the king, having supped with the Duchess de Berri, retired to bed early, complaining of weariness and exhaustion. The rumor

* Memoires de St. Simon.

spread rapidly that the king was dangerously
sick. The foreign embassadors promptly dispatched the news to their several courts.

The jealous king, who kept himself minutely informed of every thing which transpired,
was very indignant in view of this apparent
eagerness to hurry him to the tomb. To prove,
not only to the court, but to all Europe, that he
was still every inch a king, he ordered a magnificent review of the royal troops at Marly.
The trumpet of preparation was blown loudly.
Many came, not only from different parts of
the kingdom, but from the other states of Europe, to witness the spectacle. It took place
on the 20th of June, 1715. As the troops, in
their gorgeous uniforms, defiled before the terrace of Marly, quite a spruce-looking man, surrounded by obsequious attendants, emerged
from the principal entrance of the palace, descended the marble steps and mounted his
horse. It was the poor old king. Inspired by
vanity, which even dying convulsions could not
quell, he had rouged his pale and haggard
cheeks, wigged his thin locks, padded his skeleton limbs, and dressed himself in the almost
juvenile costume of earlier years. Sustained
by artificial stimulants, this poor old man kept

his tottering seat upon his saddle for four long
hours. He then, having proved that he was
still young and vigorous, returned to his chamber. The wig was thrown aside, the pads removed, the paint washed off, and the infirm
septuagenarian sought rest from his exhaustion upon the royal couch.

Day after day the king grew more feeble,
with the usual alternations of nervous strength
and debility, but with no abatement of his
chronic gloom. The struggles which he endured to conceal the approaches of decay did
but accelerate that decay. He was restless,
and again lethargic. Dropsical symptoms appeared in his discolored feet and swollen an-
kles. Still he insisted every day upon seeing
his ministers, and exhibited himself padded,
and rouged, and costumed in the highest style
of art. He even affected, in his gait and gesture, the elasticity of youth. In his restless-
ness, the king repaired, with his court, from
Marly to Versailles.

Here the king was again taken seriously sick
with an attack of fever. With unabated resolution, he continued his struggles against the
approaches of the angel of death. While the
fevered blood was throbbing in his veins, he

declared that he was but slightly indisposed,
and summoned a musical band to his presence,
with orders that the musicians should perform
only the most animating and cheerful melo-
dies.

But the fever and other alarming symptoms
increased so rapidly that scarcely had the band
been assembled when the court physicians became apprehensive that the king's dissolution
was immediately to take place. The king's
confessor and the Cardinal de Rohan were
promptly summoned to attend to the last services of the Catholic Church for the dying.
There was a scene of confusion in the palace.
The confessor, Le Tellier, communicated to the
king the intelligence that he was probably
near his end. While he was receiving the
confession of the royal penitent, the cardinal
was hurrying to the chapel to get the viaticum
for administering the communion, and the
holy oil for the rite of extreme unction.

It was customary that the *pyx*, as the box
was called in which the host was kept, should
be conveyed to the bedside of expiring royalty
in formal procession. The cardinal, in his
robes of office, led the way. Several attendants of the royal household followed, bearing

torches. Then came Madame de Maintenon.
They all gathered in the magnificent chamber,
and around the massive, sumptuous couch of
the monarch. The cardinal, after speaking a
few words in reference to the solemnity of a
dying hour, administered the sacrament and
the holy oils. The king listened reverently
and in silence, and then sank back upon his
pillow, apparently resigned to die.

To the surprise of all, he revived. Patiently
he bore his sufferings, which at times were severe. His legs began to swell badly and painfully. Mortification took place. He was informed that the amputation of the leg was
necessary to save him from speedy death.

"Will the operation prolong my life?" inquired the king.

"Yes, sire," the surgeon replied; "certainly
for some days, perhaps for several weeks."

"If that be all," said the king, "it is not
worth the suffering. God's will be done."

The king could not conceal the anguish with
which he was agitated in view of his wicked
life. He fully believed in the religion of the
New Testament, and that after death came the
judgment. He tried to believe that the priest
had power to grant him absolution from his

sins. How far he succeeded in this no one can know.

Openly he expressed his anguish in view of the profligacy of his youth, and wept bitterly in the retrospect of those excesses. We know not what compunctions of conscience visited him as he reflected upon the misery he had caused by the persecution of the Protestants. But he had been urged to this by his highest ecclesiastics, and even by the holy father himself.

It would not be strange, under these circumstances, if a man of his superstitious and fanatical spirit should, even in a dying hour, reflect with some complacency upon these crimes, believing that thus he had been doing God service. It is this which gives to papal *fanaticism* its terrible and demoniac energy. The *sincere* papist believes "*heresy*" to be poison for the soul infinitely more dreadful than any poison for the body. Such poison must be banished from the world at whatever cost of suffering. Many an ecclesiastic has gone from his closet of prayer to kindle the flames which consumed his victim. The more *sincere* the papist is in his belief, the more mercilessly will he swing the scourge and fire the fagot.

Deplorable condition of France.

Loudly, however, he deplored the madness of his ambition which had involved Europe in such desolating wars. Bitterly he expressed his regret that he left France in a state of such exhaustion, impoverished, burdened with taxation, and hopelessly crushed by debt.

The condition of the realm was indeed deplorable. A boy of five years of age was to inherit the throne. A man so profligate that he was infamous even in a court which rivaled Sodom in its corruption was to be invested with the regency of the kingdom—a man who was accused, by the general voice of the nation, of having poisoned those who stood between him and the throne. That man's sister, an unblushing wanton, who had poisoned her own husband, presided over the festivities of the palace. The nobles, abandoned to sensual indulgence, were diligent and ingenious only in their endeavors to wrench money from the poor. The masses of the people were wretched beyond description, and almost beyond imagination in our land of liberty and competence. The execrations of the starving millions were rising in a long wail around the throne.

Thomas Jefferson, subsequently President of

1—26

the United States, who, not many years after
this, was the American embassador at Paris,
wrote, in 1785, to Mrs. Trist, of Philadelphia,

" Of twenty millions of people supposed to
be in France, I am of the opinion that there
are nineteen millions more wretched, more ac-
cursed in every circumstance of human existence than the most conspicuously wretched individual of the whole United States."

Even the Duke of Orleans, the appointed
regent, said, " If I were a subject I would certainly revolt. The people are good-natured
fools to suffer so long."

These sufferings and these corruptions were
the origin and cause of the French Revolution.* Napoleon, the great advocate of the
rights of the people in antagonism to this aristocratic privilege, said, at St. Helena,

" Our Revolution was a national convulsion
as irresistible in its effects as an eruption of
Vesuvius. When the mysterious fusion which
takes place in the entrails of the earth is at
such a crisis that an explosion follows, the
eruption bursts forth. The unperceived work-
ings of the discontent of the people follow ex-

* Abbott's French Revolution, as viewed in the Light of
Republican Institutions.

actly the same course. In France, the sufferings of the people, the moral combinations
which produce a revolution, had arrived at
maturity, and the explosion took place."*

Such was the condition in which unhappy
France was left by Louis XIV., after a reign
of seventy years. He was now seventy-seven
years of age. Madame de Maintenon, two
years his senior, was entering her eightieth
year. With unwearied devotion she watched
at the bedside of that selfish husband whose
pride would never allow him to acknowledge
her publicly as his wife.

Feeling that his end was drawing near, the
king summoned the Duke of Orleans to his
bedside, and informed him minutely of the
measures he wished to have adopted after his
death. The duke listened respectfully, but
paid no more regard to the wishes of the now
powerless and dying king than to the wailing
of the wind. The king had penetration
enough to see that his day was over. He sank
back upon his pillow in despair.

On the 26th of August several prominent
members of his court were invited to the dying chamber of the king. His voice was al-

* Napoleon at St. Helena, p. 374

most gone.　He beckoned them to gather near
around his bed.　Then, in feeble tones, tremu-
lous with emotion, the pitiable old man, conscious of his summons to the tribunal of God,
said,

"Gentlemen, I ask your pardon for the bad
example I have set you.　I thank you for your
fidelity to me, and beg you to be equally faithful to my grandson.　Farewell, gentlemen.
Forgive me.　I hope you will sometimes think
of me when I am gone."

> "By many a death-bed I have been,
> By many a sinner's parting scene,
> But never aught like this."

It was, indeed, a spectacle mournfully sublime.　The dying chamber was one of the
most magnificent apartments in the palace of
Versailles.　The royal couch, massive in its
architecture, richly curtained in its embroidered upholstery of satin and gold, presented a
bed whose pillowed luxury exhibited haggard
death in the strongest possible contrast.

Upon this gorgeous bed the gray-haired king
reclined, wrinkled and wan, and with a countenance which bore the traces both of physical
suffering and of keen remorse.　The velvet
hangings of the bed were looped back with

heavy tassels of gold. A group of nobles in gorgeous court costumes were kneeling around the bed. Dispersed over the vast apartment were other groups of courtiers and ladies, in picturesque attitudes of real or affected grief. The gilded cornices, the richly-painted ceilings, the soft carpet, yielding to the pressure of the foot, the lavish display of the most costly and luxurious furniture, all conspired to render the dimmed eye, and wasted cheek, and palsied frame of the dying more impressive.

At a gesture from the king nearly all retired. For a few moments there was unbroken silence. The king then requested his great grandchild, who was to be his successor, to be brought to him. A cushion was placed by the side of the bed, and the half-frightened child, clinging to the hand of his governess, kneeled upon it. Louis XIV. gazed for a few moments with almost pitying tenderness upon the infant prince, and then said,

"My child, you are about to become a great king. Do not imitate me either in my taste for building or in my love of war. Live in peace with the nations. Render to God all that you owe him. Teach your subjects to honor His name. Strive to relieve the bur-

dens of your people, in which I have been so
unfortunate as to fail.   Never forget the gratitude you owe to the Duchess de Ventadour."*

"Madame," said the king, addressing Madame de Ventadour, " permit me to embrace
the prince."

The dauphin was placed upon the bed.
The king encircled him in his arms, pressed
him fondly to his breast, and said, in a voice
broken by emotion,

"I bless you, my dear child, with all my
heart."   He then raised his eyes to heaven,
and uttered a short prayer for God's blessing
upon the boy.

The next day, after another night of languor
and suffering, the restless, conscience-stricken
king again summoned the dignitaries of the
court to his bedside, and said to them, in the
presence of Madame de Maintenon and of his
confessor, who had mainly instigated him in
the persecution of the Protestants,

"Gentlemen, I die in the faith and obedience of the Church.   I know nothing of the

---

* The Duchess de Ventadour, by the most careful nursing,
to which she entirely devoted herself, had rescued the infant
Duke of Anjou from the effect of the poison to which his father, mother, and brother had fallen victims.

dogmas by which it is divided. I have followed the advice which I have received, and have
done only what I was desired to do. If I have
erred, my guides alone must answer before
God, whom I call upon to witness this asser-
tion."

The succeeding night the king was restless
and greatly agitated. He could not sleep, and
seemed to pass the whole night in agonizing
prayer. In the morning he said to Madame
de Maintenon,

"At this moment I only regret yourself. I
have not made you happy. But I have ever
felt for you all the regard and affection which
you deserved. My only consolation in leaving
you exists in the hope that we shall, ere long,
meet again in eternity."

Hours of agony, bodily and mental, were
still allotted to the king. His limbs were badly swollen. Upon one of them mortification
was rapidly advancing. He was often deliri-
ous, with but brief intervals of consciousness.
The service for the dying was performed.
The ceremony seemed slightly to arouse him
from his lethargy. His voice was heard occasionally blending with the prayers of the ecclesiastics as he repeated several times,

"Now, in the hour of death, O my God, come to my aid."

These were his last words. He sank back insensible upon his pillow. A few hours of painful breathing passed away, and at eight o'clock in the morning of the 1st of September, 1715, he expired, in the seventy-seventh year of his age and the seventy-second of his reign. It was the longest reign in the annals of France. Had he been governed through this period by enlightened Christian principle, how many millions might have been made happy whom his crimes doomed to life-long woe!

An immense concourse was assembled in the court-yard at Versailles, anticipating the announcement of his death. The moment he breathed his last sigh, the captain of the body-guard approached the great balcony, threw open the massive windows, and, looking down upon the multitude below, raised his truncheon above his head, broke it in the centre, threw the fragments down into the court-yard, and cried sadly, "The king is dead!"

Then, instantly seizing another staff from the hands of an attendant, he waved it joyfully above his head, and shouted triumphantly,

"Long live the king, Louis XV.!" A huzza burst from the lips of the assembled thousands almost loud enough to pierce the ear of the king, now palsied in death.

ANNOUNCEMENT OF THE DEATH OF LOUIS XIV.

There were few to mourn the departed monarch. As his remains were hurried to the vaults of St. Denis, those vaults which he had so much dreaded, the populace shouted execrations and pelted his coffin with mud. Not the

slightest regard was paid to his will. The
Duke of Orleans assumed the regency with
absolute power. His reign was execrable, followed by the still more infamous reign of
Louis XV. Then came the Revolution, as the
sceptre of utterly despotic sway passed into the
hands of the feeble Louis XVI. The storm,
which had been gathering for ages, burst with
fury which appalled the world. A more tre-
mendous event has not occurred in the history
of our race. The story has too often been
told by those who were in sympathy with the
kings and the nobles. The time will come
when the *people's* side of the story will be received, and the terrible drama will be better
understood.

THE END.

COSIMO

COSIMO is a specialty publisher of books and publications that inspire, inform, and engage readers. Our mission is to offer unique books to niche audiences around the world.

COSIMO BOOKS publishes books and publications for innovative authors, nonprofit organizations, and businesses. COSIMO BOOKS specializes in bringing books back into print, publishing new books quickly and effectively, and making these publications available to readers around the world.

COSIMO CLASSICS offers a collection of distinctive titles by the great authors and thinkers throughout the ages. At COSIMO CLASSICS timeless works find new life as affordable books, covering a variety of subjects including: Business, Economics, History, Personal Development, Philosophy, Religion & Spirituality, and much more!

COSIMO REPORTS publishes public reports that affect your world, from global trends to the economy, and from health to geopolitics.

FOR MORE INFORMATION CONTACT US AT
INFO@COSIMOBOOKS.COM

➢ if you are a book lover interested in our current catalog of books

➢ if you represent a bookstore, book club, or anyone else interested in special discounts for bulk purchases

➢ if you are an author who wants to get published

➢ if you represent an organization or business seeking to publish books and other publications for your members, donors, or customers.

COSIMO BOOKS ARE ALWAYS
AVAILABLE AT ONLINE BOOKSTORES

VISIT COSIMOBOOKS.COM
BE INSPIRED, BE INFORMED